DREAMS

YOU SHOULDN'T IGNORE

Copyright © 2024 by Ola Abina. All rights reserved.

No portion of this book may be reproduced, stored in a retrieval system, distributed, or transmitted in any form or by any means, including photocopying, recording, or other electronic or mechanical methods, without the prior written permission of the publisher, except in the case of brief quotations embodied in critical reviews or articles.

ISBN 979-8-9862426-0-6
Cover design: Jesus Is Too Real (JITR).
Published by Jesus Is Too Real (JITR).
Baltimore, Maryland
www.jesusistooreal.com

Unless otherwise noted, Scripture quotations are taken from The Holy Bible, New Living Translation (NLT), copyright ©1996, 2004, 2007, 2013 by Tyndale House Foundation. Used by permission of Tyndale House Publishers, Inc., Carol Stream, Illinois 60188. All rights reserved. Other Scripture references are from the following sources: the New King James Version®. Copyright © 1982 by Thomas Nelson. Used by permission. All rights reserved. Represented by Tyndale House Publishers, Inc. Used by permission of Baker Publishing Group the Holy Bible, New International Version®, (NIV)®. Easy-to-Read Version (ERV) Copyright © 2006 by Bible League International. Common English Bible (CEB) Copyright © 2011 by Common English Bible. Amplified Bible (AMP) Copyright © 2015 by The Lockman Foundation, La Habra, CA 90631. All rights reserved.

DREAMS

YOU SHOULDN'T IGNORE

BIBLE-BASED INTERPRETATIONS
+How To Interpret Your Difficult Dreams
+ Symbols, Signs, Colors, Numbers
+30-Day Dream Interpretation Journal

OLA ABINA

*For everyone who dares to believe
in their dreams and go after it.*

CONTENTS

INTRODUCTION	1
HOW TO USE THIS BOOK	3
CHAPTER 1: Why Interpret Your Dream?	9
CHAPTER 2: Common Dream Problems (Forgetting, Incomplete & Opposite Dreams)	15
CHAPTER 3: How To Interpret Your Dreams (Step by Step)	19
CHAPTER 4: How To Interpret Your Difficult Dreams	23
CHAPTER 5: Numbers In Dreams	31
CHAPTER 6: Colors In Dreams	41
CHAPTER 7: Animals In Dreams	47
CHAPTER 8: Birds In Dreams	65
CHAPTER 9: Fruits In Dreams	75
CHAPTER 10: Food & Drinks in Dreams	87
CHAPTER 11: Fights, Contentions & Mishaps in Dreams	99
CHAPTER 12: Exes, Past Life & Death Dreams	113
CHAPTER 13: Elevator, Watch & Phone Dreams	119
CHAPTER 14: Transportation Dreams (Cars, Plane, Train)	129
CHAPTER 15: Clothing and Shoes Dreams	139
30-DAY DREAM INTERPRETATION JOURNAL	149
BOOKS BY OLA ABINA	181
ABOUT THE AUTHOR	187

INTRODUCTION

[14] "For God speaks again and again, though people do not recognize it. [15] He speaks in dreams, in visions of the night, when deep sleep falls on people as they lie in their beds. [16] He whispers in their ears and terrifies them with warnings. [17] He makes them turn from doing wrong; he keeps them from pride." Job 33:14-17 (NLT).

"After this, I will pour out my Spirit on all kinds of people. Your sons and daughters will prophesy, your old men will have dreams, and your young men will see visions." Joel 2:28 (ERV).

From a young age, I realized I had a remarkable gift from the Lord: vivid dreams and the ability to interpret them. Initially, I paid little attention to these nightly visions, but as they began to unfold in real life, their profound significance became clear. The Lord revealed hidden truths about people, events, and situations, often confirmed by astonished reactions.

Over time, many people sought my help with their perplexing dreams. Through accurate interpretations, I witnessed miraculous transformations—lives saved from tragic accidents, early detection of diseases, healed marriages, and wise investments—all thanks to the power of dream interpretation.

Introduction

Driven by a desire to help even more people, I launched a social media series that attracted over 100,000 viewers eager for understanding. However, the demand became overwhelming, leading me to create this book. Here, I share interpretations of crucial dreams, the meanings behind common symbols and colors, and practical guidance for understanding and interpreting your own dreams.

Dreams open windows to our spirit, providing God's guidance, comfort, and revelations, as depicted in scripture. This book explores biblical dream interpretation, highlighting some dreams that should not be ignored. It helps you understand God's messages through symbolic language and parables.

Referencing dreams from the Bible, such as Joseph's (Genesis 37:5-10) and Gideon's (Daniel 2:19), this book offers practical steps for modern dreamers to interpret their difficult dreams. Whether you're seeking direction, reassurance, or a deeper spiritual connection, this book promises to enlighten and enhance your spiritual growth. By understanding and interpreting your dreams, you can align more closely with God's purpose, similar to how Solomon sought wisdom (1 Kings 3:5-15).

While the book focuses on dream interpretations, the principles can also be applied to trances, visions, and any type of spiritual revelations. My prayer is that it blesses you with the clarity and insight you seek.

HOW TO USE THIS BOOK

Do It Yourself Approach

This book helps you understand your dreams. It doesn't try to explain every possible dream or symbol. Instead, it focuses on common dreams you should pay attention to, what they mean, and what to do about them, whether they're good or bad. The examples in the book will help you compare with your own dreams and understand their importance in your life. For more dream interpretations, check out the videos I made on YouTube: DREAMS & INTERPRETATIONS."

https://youtube.com/playlist?list=PLzLMIZ_UKzt59gpHKx4iuIXXYmFF747-E&si=pfK8uGWIG5dYQ4Df .

Dreams Are to be Interpreted, Not Translated

Dreams should be interpreted, not translated. For example, when Pharaoh dreamed of seven skinny cows swallowing seven fat cows, there was no direct translation. It required interpretation to understand it meant seven years of famine (Genesis 41:17-36).

Context Matters

To properly understand your dream, consider what's happening in your life. The context helps with accurate interpretation. Interpreting a dream without context can be misleading.

From The Known

Your dreams are influenced by what you already know. For instance, if you only speak English, your dreams won't be in French. Most of what you see in dreams will be familiar to you. This helps in interpreting them. For example, Joseph's dreams in the Bible couldn't have been about modern things like airplanes or the internet.

Junk

"A hungry person dreams of eating but wakes up still hungry. A thirsty person dreams of drinking but is still faint from thirst when morning comes..." Isaiah 29:8.

Sometimes dreams mix meaningful scenes with irrelevant ones. Dreams can be influenced by many factors, including your thoughts and physical state. If you're hungry or thirsty, you might dream of eating or drinking.

Isolation

To accurately interpret dreams, focus on the main theme and ignore irrelevant details.

Book Organization

Dream

Each chapter starts with a common dream, categorized by themes like animals or fruits. Sometimes, variations of dreams are included if their meanings differ significantly.

Interpretation

Following the dream, possible interpretations are presented, often based on scripture. If no scriptural examples exist, the interpretations are done by inspiration and drawing on years of experience. For example, dreaming about riding a train or car isn't in scripture but generally symbolizes a life journey.

What To Do

Next are suggested actions based on the interpretation. Choose the ones that apply to your situation.

Prayer Points (Warfare Prayers)

"14 Stand therefore, having girded your waist with truth, having put on the breastplate of righteousness, 15 and having shod your feet with the preparation of the gospel of peace; 16 above all, taking the shield of faith with which you will be able to quench all the fiery darts of the wicked one. 17 And take the helmet of salvation, and the sword of the Spirit, which is the word of God; 18 praying always with all prayer and supplication in the Spirit, being watchful to this end with all perseverance and supplication for all the saints—" Ephesians 6:14-18 (NKJV).

After "What To Do," you'll find Prayer Points, designed to help you overcome in the spiritual realm.

Since dreams are part of the spiritual realm, you need spiritual tools to influence them. One of the most powerful tools is prayer. Many of these prayers are warfare prayers because, according to the Bible, we are constantly fighting against the enemy. The prayers are meant to be strong and determined. To defeat the devil and his agents, we must use the right tools. Even if you don't fully understand them, I suggest praying them and letting God handle the rest. These prayers are effective. Use them to secure good dreams or overturn bad ones.

Scriptures

Throughout this book, you'll find related scriptures. Reading them will build your faith and conviction, which are essential for effective prayer and for God to respond. God is moved by faith according to Hebrews 11:6.

What To Know

The Enemy

"Be sober, be vigilant; because your adversary the devil walks about like a roaring lion, seeking whom he may devour." 1 Peter 5:8. (NKJV)

In this book, the "enemy" refers to Satan, the ultimate adversary of every human being, especially believers (John 10:10). He is pure evil, relentless, and can never be pacified—only resisted (James 4:7). Satan is invisible but highly organized, operating from the spiritual realm, which includes dreams, to impose his will on humans and the world. He carries out his evil plans through different levels, as described in Ephesians 6:12: *"For we do not wrestle against flesh and blood, but against principalities, against powers, against the rulers of the darkness of this age, against spiritual hosts of wickedness in the heavenly places." (NKJV)*

Skewed Interpretations

You might notice that many common dreams in this book have negative interpretations. This is intentional, based on years of handling dream requests. If bad dreams are not properly interpreted and nothing is done about them, they could cause serious, irreversible harm. Bad dreams can affect you if you do nothing.

Authority In the Spiritual Realm

For the recommended solutions, including prayers to be effective, you need a personal relationship with our Lord Jesus Christ. It is through His authority that we can control what happens on earth, in heaven, and beyond (Matthew 18:18).

If you don't have a personal relationship with Jesus Christ, you can establish it now by saying the following: "Lord Jesus, come into my heart as my Lord and Savior. Forgive me my sins. I confess my sins of _____ (name them). I believe that You are the Son of God. I confess that You are my Lord and Savior from today. Thank You. Amen."

Once you've done this, God will answer your prayers.

CHAPTER 1

Why Interpret Your Dream?

Why should you have your dreams interpreted? With this beginning chapter we will explore why you should know and understand the meaning of your dreams.

1. Communication From God

One of the reasons to have your dreams interpreted is to understand communications from God. God, the Father of spirits, meaning human beings (Hebrews 12:9), naturally communicates with the spirit of man in the spiritual realm (world). The dream world is one of those spiritual realms, and you are primarily a spirit, with a soul, living in a body. *"And the LORD God formed man of the dust of the ground, and breathed into his nostrils the breath of life; and man became a living soul." Genesis 2:7 (KJV).*

Why Interpret Your Dream?

Regrettably, even though mankind is a spirit, the spirit part of man is the least understood and most often despised. One of the reasons is because it is difficult to understand the things of the spirit.

"For God speaks again and again, though people do not recognize it. He speaks in dreams, in visions of the night, when deep sleep falls on people as they lie in their beds. He whispers in their ears and terrifies them with warnings. He makes them turn from doing wrong; he keeps them from pride." Job 33:14-17.

2. Bad Seeds Are Sown In Dreams

Besides God speaking to us in dreams, Satan, our main enemy, also uses dreams to spread evil through his agents. They plant harmful seeds while we sleep. As the Bible says in Matthew 13:25 (NKJV): *"but while men slept, his enemy came and sowed tares among the wheat and went his way."* They do this because people are most vulnerable when they're asleep. Often, it takes careful interpretation to realize this has happened.

3. The More Difficult Your Dream, The More Important

If your dream is hard to understand, it usually means it's very important for your life. For example, in the Bible, King Pharaoh had dreams of seven skinny cows swallowing seven fat cows and seven thin heads of grain swallowing seven plump heads of grain (Genesis 41:1-36). These dreams were tough to interpret, but they were crucial for the survival of Egypt. Not understanding your dreams doesn't protect you from their consequences.

4. The Dream World Is Superior to The Physical World

Gideon

"Gideon crept up just as a man was telling his companion about a dream. The man said, "I had this dream, and in my dream, a loaf of barley bread came tumbling down into the Midianite camp. It hit a tent, turned it over,

DREAMS

and knocked it flat!" His companion answered, "Your dream can mean only one thing—God has given Gideon son of Joash, the Israelite, victory over Midian and all its allies!"* Judges 7:13-14.

The dream world, a spiritual realm, is superior to the physical world. Whatever happens in the spiritual realm determines and influences the physical world. If you succeed in the spirit realm, you will enjoy the physical realm. If you are defeated in the spirit realm, it will manifest physically. An example was when Gideon's 300 soldiers faced over 120,000 enemy troops. A Midianite soldier's dream indicated that Gideon and his troops would defeat them despite being outnumbered (Judges 7:13-14).

5. Your Dream Can Warn Or Instruct You

Your dream could be a matter of life or death for you or your loved ones. In the Bible, a dream saved Joseph and baby Jesus from King Herod's attempt to kill them (Matthew 2:13). Ignoring such dreams can lead to premature death, while heeding them can lead to safety. Dreams can guide you to delay a journey, stay home, or take a different route to avoid danger.

6. Your Dream Can Guide You To Riches

One powerful reason to interpret your dreams is that they could lift you out of poverty or bring you great wealth.

King Solomon

King Solomon became the richest man ever because of a dream. *"That night the Lord appeared to Solomon in a dream, and God said, 'What do you want? Ask, and I will give it to you!' So God replied...I will give you what you asked for! I will give you a wise and understanding heart such as no one else has had or ever will have! And I will also give you what you did not ask for—riches and fame! No other king in all the world will be compared to you for the rest of your life! Then Solomon woke up and realized it had been a dream..."* (1 Kings 3:5, 11-13, 15). God still gives such dreams today.

Madam C.J. Walker

A modern example is Madam C.J. Walker, the first African American millionairess. She credited her very successful hair product to a dream. "A big black man appeared to me and told me what to mix up for my hair. Some of the remedy was grown in Africa, but I sent for it, put it on my scalp, and in a few weeks my hair was coming in faster than it had ever fallen out."

Larry Page

Larry Page, one of the co-founders of Google (Alphabet), had a dream at 23 about building Google and how to download the entire internet with links. He said, "When I suddenly woke up…I grabbed a pen and started writing." Today, 28 years later, that idea from the dream is now worth over $2 trillion. Larry Page's personal fortune is worth over $136 billion.

7. Your Dream Can Tell You Your Future

God can use your dreams to reveal your future. These are called prophetic dreams because they foretell what is to come. In the Bible, Joseph, son of Jacob (Israel), had several dreams that predicted his future. Once he interpreted them, he knew he was destined to be a ruler. God still gives such dreams today.

"Soon Joseph had another dream, and again he told his brothers about it. 'Listen, I have had another dream,' he said. 'The sun, moon, and eleven stars bowed low before me!' This time he told the dream to his father as well as to his brothers, but his father scolded him. 'What kind of dream is that?' he

asked. 'Will your mother and I and your brothers actually come and bow to the ground before you?'" (Genesis 37:9-10).

8. Your Dream Can Answer Your Prayers

If you have prayed to God about something, He might answer you through a dream. For example, King Solomon prayed to God, and God answered him in a dream. *"Then the Lord appeared to Solomon a second time, as he had done before at Gibeon. The Lord said to him, 'I have heard your prayer and your petition...'" (1 Kings 9:2-3).*

God still answers prayers through dreams today. He doesn't need to physically appear in your dreams for you to know He's answered your prayers. He might use symbols or send a well-known person you respect to give you directions in your dream. It could also be an angel.

CHAPTER 2

Common Dream Problems (Forgetting, Incomplete & Opposite Dreams)

In this chapter, we'll discuss common dream problems like forgetting dreams, incomplete dreams, and dreaming of something but experiencing the opposite. I'll also share tips on how to take care of your dreams.

Forgetting Dreams

Forgetting your dreams can sometimes be due to stress and fatigue. However, if you constantly forget your dreams, it might be a Satanic attack. The enemy tries to keep you in ignorance, afflict you, or cause stagnation. If you remember a dream about a solution to a problem you're facing, you might take action to make it happen. The enemy steals that dream to keep you bound.

What to Do

- Pray the following prayers to see a change.

Prayer Points

1. I invoke the blood of Jesus against every Satanic attack stealing my dreams. Stop now.
2. I invoke the blood of Jesus against every witchcraft attack stealing my dreams. Stop now.
3. Father, in the name of Jesus, by Your Holy Spirit, bring to my remembrance every forgotten dream relevant to my life.

Incomplete Dreams

Sometimes dreams are incomplete because external factors like loud noises or sudden lights interrupt them. Your dream could also be interrupted if someone wakes you up. Additionally, dreams can be spiritually manipulated to be incomplete. Important elements might be cut off, or noises in the dream could prevent you from hearing key instructions. An agent of the enemy might also disrupt your dream.

What to Do

- Talk to God to bring back the dream.
- Ask God for the ability to restart your dreams.
- Ask God to continue the dream from where you left off.
- Pray against witchcraft activities.

Prayer Points

1. Thank you, Father, for loving me with everything.
2. Father, in the name of Jesus, by Your Holy Spirit, bring back incomplete dreams that are important for my life.
3. Father, in the name of Jesus, by Your Holy Spirit, give me the ability to restart incomplete dreams that are important for my life.
4. Father, in the name of Jesus, by Your Holy Spirit, give me the ability to continue incomplete dreams that are important for my life.
5. I invoke the blood of Jesus against every witchcraft and sorcery attack disrupting my dreams. Stop now.

Opposite Dreams

Some people experience the opposite of their dreams. If this happens to you, it indicates demonic manipulation. The enemy hijacks your dreams and plants spiritual weeds, causing the opposite outcome. This can make you despise good dreams, perpetuating a cycle of bad experiences.

What to Do

- Pray the following prayers with fasting for at least three consecutive nights.

Prayer Points

1. Thank You, Father, because You will do what I ask in Jesus' name (John 14:14).
2. In the name of Jesus, I uproot every spiritual weed sown into my dream life that contends with my good dreams.
3. In the name of Jesus, I uproot every spiritual tree of opposites sown into my dream life that contends with my good dreams.
4. In the name of Jesus, I command the fire of God against every demonic agent manipulating my dream life.

5. I invoke the blood of Jesus against every witchcraft and sorcery attack giving me opposite dreams. Stop now (Revelation 12:11).

Taking Care of Your Dreams

Your dreams are important and should be well taken care of. Dreams can be instructional, informational, cautionary, prophetic, affirming, or answers to prayers. They can also be influenced by the devil, stem from your own desires, or be meaningless. Always take your dreams seriously and pray about them.

Tips for Taking Care of Your Dreams

1. Keep a pen and pad next to your bed to write down your dreams. If you prefer, use your phone in dark mode or record your dreams orally.
2. After dreaming, keep your eyes closed as you wake up.
3. Ensure the lights are off and there are no sudden sounds or movements. Dreams are sensitive to light, sound, and movement.
4. With your eyes closed, try to recall your dream from start to finish without adding any meaning.
5. Rehearse your dream mentally to save it for later recollection.
6. Once you can recollect your dream, open your eyes.
7. Write down your dream in its entirety. If using your phone, resist the temptation to engage in other tasks.

CHAPTER 3

How To Interpret Your Dreams (Step by Step)

This book aims to help you understand your own dreams so you can take beneficial actions.

To interpret your dreams accurately, you need to see yourself as unique. Even though we're all human, our DNA is different. For example, a hereditary disease in one family might not affect their neighbors or friends.

Everyone also has a different destiny and purpose. This means your dreams will be unique to you and should influence how you approach life. For instance, if you have an allergy, you take special precautions. The same goes for your spiritual life; you may need to adjust certain areas where you face challenges.

How To Interpret Your Dreams (Step by Step)

When interpreting dreams, follow the steps outlined in the book. Use the meanings of numbers, colors, animals, and objects as a guide if needed.

Steps:

1. First, note your initial reaction or impression when you woke up from your dream. Were you joyful, excited, or afraid and confused? Note this, as it is one of the pieces to piecing the meaning of your dream together, especially whether it is a good or bad dream. The initial impression is important because it has not been tainted or swayed by your consciousness.
2. Begin the process of isolation and elimination.
3. Does your dream have a main concept or action that occurred? The main theme or concept could be identified by what all the actions or inactions were leading to.
4. If it does, who performed the action or didn't act? Was it you or someone else?
5. What were you or the person doing or not doing?
6. What was the outcome of the dream? How did it end—victory, defeat, uncertainty, success, or failure?
7. Are there numbers written or mentioned? Or were quantities referenced, for example, three chairs?
8. Were there colors written, mentioned, worn, or seen, for example, a red dress?
9. Were there animals?
10. Were there objects?
11. Identify what is currently going on in your life that could provide context for the dream.

DREAMS

Once you have interpreted your dream, proceed to the steps for action below. How do you identify the actions you should take? Follow the steps below.

Steps for Action: View your dreams through the following lens:

1. Is this dream an answer to a prayer that I had prayed? Note it.
2. Is this dream a result of a worry or concern that is weighing on my mind? Note it.
3. Is this dream futuristic? Is it a foretelling of what is to come? Document and keep it.
4. Is this dream related to current events in my life or others? Investigate more if needed.
5. Is this dream related to something that happened in the past? Check if there are symptoms.
6. Is there a warning or symbols of warnings in this dream? Document it.
7. Is there a direct or indirect instruction or symbols of such in this dream that I need to follow? Note it.
8. Is this a recurring bad dream? That means I have not sufficiently addressed it or am applying the wrong solution.
9. Is this a recurring good dream? That means I have an assurance from God that He will fulfill His good thoughts towards me.

If you are unable to interpret your dream decisively after following the above steps, read the next chapter: "How To Interpret Your Difficult Dreams."

CHAPTER 4

How To Interpret Your Difficult Dreams

In this chapter, we'll explore how to interpret difficult dreams. Before diving into this, it's a good idea to first read the previous chapter, "How To Interpret Your Dreams (Step by Step)" and use it along with this one.

General Interpretation

Most of your dreams should have straightforward meanings. If they don't, familiarize yourself with the meanings of numbers, animals, objects, colors, and other symbols explained in the book. This should help you. However, some dreams may still not have a clear meaning and may not fit neatly into these categories.

Focus on Actions

Sometimes, a dream is hard to interpret because the object or subject can't be easily understood. In such cases, focus not on the object or subject itself but on the actions performed or being performed that determined the outcome of the dream. Sometimes, even inaction provides clues to a dream's meaning.

Context Matters

Next, interpret your dream in the context of what's happening in your life. The best interpretation will always be based on your current circumstances. Avoid interpreting dreams outside the context of who you are and what's going on in your life.

Let's use the example of a Midianite's dream during Gideon's time. This was how Gideon received confirmation from God to fight the Midianites. You can read the full story in the book of Judges, chapter seven.

1. A Midianite's Dream Example

"Gideon crept up just as a man was telling his companion about a dream. The man said, 'I had this dream, and in my dream a loaf of barley bread came tumbling down into the Midianite camp. It hit a tent, turned it over, and knocked it flat!'" Judges 7:13.

Understanding the Dream

At first glance, interpreting this dream can be challenging. A loaf of barley bread rolling into a camp and knocking down tents might sound like a child's dream. But the dream was far from meaningless. Let's break it down to see how it applies to difficult dreams.

DREAMS

Context

"Soon afterward, the armies of Midian, Amalek, and the people of the east formed an alliance against Israel and crossed the Jordan, camping in the valley of Jezreel. Then the Spirit of the Lord clothed Gideon with power. He blew a ram's horn as a call to arms, and the men of the clan of Abiezer came to him. He also sent messengers throughout Manasseh, Asher, Zebulun, and Naphtali, summoning their warriors, and all of them responded." (Judges 6:33-35).

To understand a dream, start with the context. Consider what is happening in your life. In this example, the Midianites and Amalekites had allied against Israel. Gideon rallied the Israelites to fight. Both sides were aware of their opposition. The alliance camped in tents, awaiting instructions to attack.

Action or Inaction

Focus on the main action or inaction that determines the dream's outcome. When an army's tent is knocked over and laid flat, it signals defeat. The Midianites' camp being knocked over indicates they would be attacked and defeated.

Identifying the Subject

The dream's subject was a loaf of barley bread, which might not seem significant. Normally, bread isn't associated with a human being in a dream, but in this dream, it symbolizes something else.

To uncover what the loaf of barley bread represents, identify who the Midianites are opposing: the Israelites. Who leads the Israelites? Gideon. This suggests that Gideon is represented by the loaf of barley bread.

Conclusion

How could a loaf of barley bread knock down the tents of the mighty Midianite army, along with the Amalekites and people of the east? It signifies that something or someone physically insignificant, like Gideon with his 300 men, would defeat an army of over 120,000 (Judges 8:10).

2. Previous Dream Connection or Similarities?

Another method for interpreting a difficult dream is to consider if you have had a similar dream before. If so, identify the connections or similarities and write them down. You can use the dream interpretation journal provided to document your dreams.

Let's use the example of Joseph's dreams in the Bible.

Dreams

First Dream (Sheaves): *"Joseph had a dream, and when he told it to his brothers, they hated him all the more. He said to them, 'Listen to this dream I had: We were binding sheaves of grain out in the field when suddenly my sheaf rose and stood upright, while your sheaves gathered around mine and bowed down to it.' His brothers said to him, 'Do you intend to reign over us? Will you actually rule us?' And they hated him all the more because of his dream and what he had said." Genesis 37:5-8. (NIV)*

Sheaves: In this dream, Joseph's sheaf stood upright while his brothers' sheaves bowed down. Normally, sheaves represent harvest or plenty, not human beings. However, Joseph likely saw eleven sheaves, representing his brothers bowing to him. His brothers understood this, realizing it meant Joseph would one day rise above them.

Second Dream (Constellations): *"Then he had another dream, and he told it to his brothers. 'Listen,' he said, 'I had another dream, and this time* *the sun and moon and eleven stars were bowing down to me.' When he told his father as well as his brothers, his father rebuked him and said, 'What is this dream you had? Will your mother and I and your brothers actually come and bow down to the ground before you?' His brothers were jealous of him, but his father kept the matter in mind."* Genesis 37:9-10. (NIV)

Stars & Similarities

In this second dream, the sun, moon, and eleven stars bowed down to Joseph. By isolating this dream and using context, we can see that the eleven stars represent Joseph's brothers. Stars represent people or their glory, as seen in the story of Jesus' star guiding the wise men (Matthew 2:2). This dream matches the first one, with Joseph's brothers bowing to him.

Sun & Moon: Additionally, the sun and moon likely represent Joseph's parents. The sun (father) and moon (mother) have greater glory than the stars. Although Joseph's mother, Rachel, had passed away by this time, dreams are symbolic and not literal. Joseph's stepmother could also be considered his mother.

Conclusion

The key similarity in both dreams is the action: the symbols bowing to Joseph. This indicates that, over time, Joseph would rise to a position of authority over his family. The repetition of the dream signifies that it was ordained by God and bound to happen.

3. Isolation and Elimination

Another method for interpreting dreams is isolation and elimination. Most dreams contain a lot of unnecessary information or "junk." The goal is not to interpret every detail but to focus on what is important and relevant. Some parts of a dream may have no significance. Sometimes, the crucial information is at the beginning of the dream, with the rest being filler. Other times, it might be in the middle or end. If a dream is difficult to interpret, it often holds significant importance for your life. Do not panic, you can still find a solution.

Example: Bill asked me online about the meaning of his dream: "I dreamed that my younger self told my older self to buy Bitcoin. Later I saw that I started fighting with everyone in my office."

Interpretation

Context

To interpret Bill's dream, we need to consider his life context. Bill might be eager to improve his financial situation and has been praying for guidance. Currently, there are no issues at his office.

Action (Isolate & Eliminate)

Given the financial context, we can eliminate the part of the dream involving office conflict as irrelevant. This leaves the focus on the advice to buy Bitcoin.

Conclusion

Bill's dream suggests he should consider investing in Bitcoin for the long term, as it may be a profitable venture for him.

Disclaimer. This is not an endorsement of Bitcoin or any investment. The interpretation is based on the information provided. If additional details were withheld or altered, the outcome of the dream could change.

4. Prayer

If you have a dream that's difficult to understand or interpret, try using the methods mentioned: look at the actions, check for similar dreams, and use the isolation and elimination strategy. Don't forget to use your dream journal to record your dreams. If you still can't interpret your dream, pray to the Lord for guidance (Daniel 2:17-19). You can pray like this: "Father, thank You for this dream. I am grateful. Father, by Your Holy Spirit, speak to my heart. Holy Spirit, think through my thoughts, and bring the accurate interpretation of this dream to me. Thank You for answering me in Jesus' name." Then try to interpret the dream again.

CHAPTER 5

Numbers In Dreams

God is intentional and deliberate about whatever He does. Nothing is random or thoughtless. Everything has significance. This includes numbers. Using numbers is one of the prominent and notable ways that God communicates. Therefore, you should be aware of the meaning of numbers from God's perspective. Throughout the Bible, we see numbers and their significance by what they are associated with. We will discuss a few numbers and their significance. If they appear in your dream, note them. This should give you clarity and further ensure that your dream interpretation is accurate.

#0 - Stagnation, Emptiness, Nothingness

The number "0" usually means stagnation, emptiness, or nothingness. For example, if you see "0" in a dream regarding your business, it implies that it is stagnant spiritually.

#1 - God, Excellence, Preeminence, Promotion

The number "1" stands for God. The Bible says in Genesis 1:1, *"In the beginning God created the heavens and the earth."* God is the first and the last. He is the Alpha (the beginning) and Omega (the end) (Revelation 22:13). He has preeminence in everything. Thus, any dream you may have that has the number one identified and prominent talks about God. Seeing number one in your dream could also mean promotion, leadership, or preeminence for you.

#2 - Multiplication, Union, Agreement, & Confirmation

The number "2" usually stands for multiplication, agreement, and confirmation.

- **Multiplication:** After the Lord created Adam and Eve (two people), He told them to be fruitful and multiply (Genesis 1:28). Also, when God was about to destroy the world, He told Noah to select a pair of each animal, male and female (Genesis 6:19). The human beings on the boat were also in pairs: Noah and his wife, and his three sons and their wives. The pairs of human beings and animals were to multiply after the flood and replenish the earth.
- **Agreement:** *"Can two walk together, unless they are agreed?" Amos 3:3. (NKJV)* The number "2" also stands for agreement. Our Lord said, *"For where two or three are gathered together in My name, I am there in the midst of them." Matthew 18:20. (NKJV)*
- **Confirmation:** The number two also stands for confirmation. Joseph confirmed to Pharaoh that his dreams would happen

because they were repeated twice. *"And the dream was repeated to Pharaoh twice because the thing is established by God, and God will shortly bring it to pass." Genesis 41:32.* Our Lord Jesus also spoke about confirming a matter: *"...take with you one or two more, that 'by the mouth of two or three witnesses every word may be established." Matthew 18:16. (NKJV)*

How could this apply to you? For example, if you are asking the Lord whether you should start a particular business or if a relationship is from Him, you could see number "2" stand out repetitively to you.

#3 - Divinity, Trinity, Triune Nature of God (Father, Son, Holy Spirit)

The number "3" represents the triune nature of God: the Father, Son, and Holy Spirit. *"For there are three that bear witness in heaven: the Father, the Word, and the Holy Spirit; and these three are one." 1 John 5:7. (NKJV)* In some cases, it could also refer to the tripartite nature of man: body, soul, and spirit.

Whenever this number is prominent, it means the triune nature of God is involved. For example, when Jesus was baptized, the triune nature of God was involved (Matthew 3:16-17). Jesus' resurrection on the third day is another indication of the involvement of God in operation. Wherever you see this number prominent, it means God is involved.

#4 - Balance, Stability, The World

The number "4" means balance and stability. For example, some things like automobiles and chairs need four "legs" to be balanced or stable.

The number four also means the world. For example, there are four corners of the earth: North, South, East, and West. *"He will send his angels with the sound of a great trumpet, and they will gather his chosen ones from the four corners of the earth, from one end of the sky to the other." Matthew 24:31. (CEB)* It could also mean the four elements: earth, wind, water, and fire.

Most importantly, seeing the number "4" could mean that God is bringing balance and stability into your life.

#5 - Grace

The number "5" represents the grace of God. If you see the number "5" in your dream or standing out to you anywhere, it is a reminder of God's grace over your life. Although not explicitly stated in the Bible, it has been understood through God's experiential dealings with man that the number "5" signifies the grace of God. The word "grace" also has five letters.

#6 - Man (Human Being), Weakness, Carnality, Mortality, Insufficiency, Beast

"Here is wisdom. Let the person who has enough insight calculate the number of the beast, for it is the [imperfect] number of a man; and his number is six hundred and sixty-six." Revelation 13:18. (AMP)

The number "6" represents man or human beings. It also refers to the frailty, weakness, or imperfection of human beings. For example, man was created on the sixth day of creation (Genesis 1:26). This is a day shy of the seventh day (perfection).

If you see this number prominent, it could mean that you are relying on human abilities, and they would fail you. You need to bring God into the situation.

#7 - Perfection, Holiness, Rest, Completion

"On the seventh day God had finished his work of creation, so he rested from all his work. And God blessed the seventh day and declared it holy, because it was the day when he rested from all his work of creation." Genesis 2:2-3.

"So Naaman went down to the Jordan River and dipped himself seven times, as the man of God had instructed him. And his skin became as healthy as the skin of a young child, and he was healed!" 2 Kings 5:14.

If you see the number "7" in your dream, it represents perfection, completion, the end of a cycle, season, or pattern. For example, on the seventh day of creation, God rested, marking the end of creation. Another instance is Naaman, who was told to dip himself in the Jordan River seven times to end his leprosy and perfect his health.

When Joseph interpreted the dream of Pharaoh, the seven heads of healthy grain and seven healthy cows represented seven years of plenty. In contrast, the seven thin heads of grain and seven skinny cows symbolized seven years of famine. Each instance of the number seven represented the end of a season or an era.

If you see the number "7" in your dream, think of the interpretation in the aforementioned context.

#8 - A New Beginning, Fresh Start

"Those who disobeyed God long ago when God waited patiently while Noah was building his boat. Only eight people were saved from drowning in that terrible flood." 1 Peter 3:20.

"Josiah was eight years old when he became king, and he reigned in Jerusalem thirty-one years. He did what was pleasing in the Lord's sight and followed the example of his ancestor David. He did not turn away from doing what was right. During the eighth year of his reign, while he was still young, Josiah began to seek the God of his ancestor David. Then in the twelfth year he began to purify Judah and Jerusalem, destroying all the pagan shrines, the Asherah poles, and the carved idols and cast images." 2 Chronicles 34:1-3.

The number "8" represents a new beginning. After the number seven, God starts over. For example, in Genesis chapter 8, God began afresh with humanity through Noah. Noah was the eighth person from Adam (Luke 3:36-38). In this fresh start, God used eight individuals—Noah, his wife, his three sons, and their wives—to start the new beginning of human beings after the completion of the flood.

Seeing the number "8" means a new beginning for you.

#9 - Manifestation, Bringing Forth, End of a Journey, Spiritual Pregnancy, Gifts of the Spirit, Fruit of the Spirit

"Do I bring to the moment of birth and not give delivery?" says the Lord. "Do I close up the womb when I bring to delivery?" says your God. "Rejoice with Jerusalem and be glad for her, all you who love her; rejoice greatly with her, all you who mourn over her. For you will nurse and be satisfied at her comforting breasts; you will drink deeply and delight in her overflowing abundance." Isaiah 66:9-11. (NIV)

The number "9" symbolizes the end of a journey and anticipation of manifestation. Therefore, if you have been working on something or believing God for something for a while, your moment of celebration is around the corner.

The number "9" in your dream also implies that you are pregnant with ideas or visions. This means you have some things in the seed stage that are about to manifest.

Also, seeing the number nine could mean that God is communicating to you to wait until the fullness of time before disclosing your next steps or moving forward.

Depending on the context of what is going on in your life, it could also symbolize the activity of the Holy Spirit in your life. There are nine fruits of the Holy Spirit (Galatians 5:22-23) and nine gifts of the Holy Spirit (1 Corinthians 12).

DREAMS

#10 - Judgment, God's Portion, Responsibility, Victory

"Should people cheat God? Yet you have cheated me! "But you ask, 'What do you mean? When did we ever cheat you?' "You have cheated me of the tithes and offerings due to me. You are under a curse, for your whole nation has been cheating me." Malachi 3:8-9.

Depending on what's happening in your life, the number "10" might represent your duty to God, which could bring consequences if not followed. For example, God gave the Israelites the Ten Commandments and breaking them could lead to God's judgment. When Solomon disobeyed God, He split the twelve tribes of Israel into two groups: Israel (ten tribes) and Judah (two tribes) (1 Kings 12:24).

The number "10" might also mean you're toying with something that belongs to God and need to repent, or face consequences. For example, Pharaoh got ten plagues because he was interfering with God's chosen people, the Israelites. God called them His firstborn.

In everything God gives us, a part belongs to Him. For instance, tithes (ten percent) are God's, and in Malachi 3:8-10, He cursed the Israelites for taking His tithes. Similarly, in the Garden of Eden, Adam and Eve weren't supposed to eat from the tree of Knowledge of Good & Evil. When they did, it brought judgment.

Finally, the number "10" could also mean God is giving you victory over challenges.

#11 - Disorder, Rebellion, Confusion, Incompleteness, Imbalance

The number "11" stands for disorder, chaos, rebellion, and confusion, going against God's perfect will. For example, in Genesis chapter 11, the story of the Tower of Babel shows people defying God's plan to spread out

Numbers In Dreams

and fill the earth, choosing instead to stay in one place, which led to confusion.

Another example is Jacob's eleven sons who sold their brother Joseph into slavery, causing imbalance against God's plan of twelve tribes of Israel.

Similarly, Jesus had twelve disciples meant to become apostles, but they were reduced to eleven after Judas Iscariot's betrayal, causing incompleteness and imbalance. The disciples later chose Matthias to restore balance.

Seeing the number eleven could mean you've deviated from God's path for you. It's a reminder to realign with God.

#12 - Kingship, Authority, Government, Rulership, Chosen

"These are the twelve tribes of Israel, and this is what their father said as he told his sons good-bye. He blessed each one with an appropriate message." Genesis 49:28.

"And when it was day, He called His disciples to Himself; and from them He chose twelve whom He also named apostles." Luke 6:13. (NKJV)

If you see the number "12" in your dreams, it symbolizes authority, leadership, and governance. It can also mean you are chosen to start something new and leave the past behind. For instance, Jacob's twelve sons became the twelve tribes of Israel, and Jesus chose twelve disciples, giving them authority and starting a new covenant with people. If you see the number "12," it might mean you are meant to bring about change or break a cycle in your family.

#24 - Higher Level of Authority, Relating To God's Majesty

The number "24" represents a higher level of authority because it's a multiple of "12," which stands for authority, leadership, and governance. So, "24" means an even greater level of these qualities, often connected to

DREAMS

God's supreme power. For example, King David organized the priests and musicians in the temple into twenty-four groups (1 Chronicles 23-24).

In Psalms 24, David talks about God's ultimate authority over the earth. And in Revelation 4:10, the Bible mentions twenty-four elders wearing crowns who worship God, highlighting His power and authority.

#30 - Beginning of A Calling, Dedication, Prophetic Fulfillment

"Jesus was about thirty years old when he began his public ministry..." Luke 3:23

"List all the men between the ages of thirty and fifty who are eligible to serve in the Tabernacle." Numbers 4:3.

"This fulfilled the prophecy of Jeremiah that says, 'They took the thirty pieces of silver—the price at which he was valued by the people of Israel,'" Matthew 27:9.

If you see the number "30" in your dream, it might mean the start of a calling from God. It could also mean God is asking you to dedicate yourself. For example, during Moses' time, men started serving in the Tabernacle at age thirty, but they had to dedicate themselves to be ready for service. Similarly, Jesus began His ministry at thirty, leaving behind His previous life to focus on His calling.

The number "30" could also symbolize the fulfillment of prophecy. For instance, Jesus was betrayed for thirty pieces of silver, fulfilling the prophecy from Zechariah (Zechariah 11:12) and Jeremiah.

#39 - Diseases, Sicknesses

"...and by His stripes we are healed." Isaiah 53:5 (NKJV).

"who Himself bore our sins in His own body on the tree, that we, having died to sins, might live for righteousness—by whose stripes you were healed." 1 Peter 2:24 (NKJV)

The number "39" represents sicknesses or diseases. For example, our Lord Jesus was given thirty-nine stripes or lashes so that we could be healed.

If you see this number in your dream, it could mean the healing of a disease or sickness in your life or that of a loved one.

#40 - Trials, Temptations, Tests, Self-Denial

"For forty days and forty nights he fasted and became very hungry." Matthew 4:2.

"Then Moses disappeared into the cloud as he climbed higher up the mountain. He remained on the mountain forty days and forty nights." Exodus 24:18.

The number "40" symbolizes trials, temptations, self-denial, and tests from God to grow spiritually.

If you see the number "40," it might mean God is preparing you for a test or letting you know you're in a period of trials. You may need to endure some difficulties, like waiting for answers to your prayers.

The number "40" also represents preparation for a calling. For instance, Moses spent forty years in the wilderness before leading the Israelites out of Egypt. He fasted for forty days twice, each time receiving guidance from God. Elijah traveled to God's mountain without food or drink for forty days and nights. Jesus fasted for forty days and nights before starting His ministry.

After these trials, you should have a closer relationship with God.

CHAPTER 6

Colors In Dreams

In addition to numbers, colors are also particularly important in dreams. God uses colors to communicate different messages. What colors have you seen in your dreams? Do you understand them?

Sometimes we pray to God on certain issues, and we dream of seeing certain colors. Since we do not know their meanings, we continue asking the Lord in prayers, not knowing that He already answered in a dream. Let's examine some colors and what they may mean in your dreams.

Red: Blood of Jesus, Love of God, Salvation, Atonement, Blood, Covenant, Jesus

(Ephesians 1:7, Colossians 1:20)

If you see red in your dream, it usually means blood and can symbolize the blood of Jesus, salvation, atonement, the love of God, and Jesus himself.

If you've sinned and are struggling to forgive yourself, seeing red in your dream means the Lord has forgiven you. If you're feeling confused or lonely, this dream reminds you of God's unfailing love.

However, seeing red or blood can also indicate a negative covenant at work. For example, if you're praying to break negative patterns in your family and see a red cloth or the killing of an animal with blood, it means there's a negative covenant causing these issues that need to be broken.

If you dream of yourself or a loved one with an injury or blood, it's a sign to pray intensely against danger or death.

Yellow: Faith, The Glory of God, The Anointing, The Holy Spirit

Yellow signifies the anointing of God. Notice how the oil for anointing has a yellowish color to it. So, if you see yellow in your dream, depending on the context, it could signify empowerment by the Holy Spirit. It could also mean the glory of God on your life. Additionally, since one of the symbols of the Holy Spirit is oil, which is yellow, it also signifies the presence of the Holy Spirit in your life.

Gold: Prosperity, Glory, Asset, Valuable, Majesty

Gold represents something valuable, majestic, and glorious. It signifies prosperity from God. If you see gold in your dream, it is a good sign from the Lord of good success. For example, if you are praying to the Lord to know if a business is worth pursuing and you see this, the Lord is telling you to go ahead. Your efforts will result in prosperity.

White: Holiness, Righteousness, Peace, Glory of God*

"I watched as thrones were put in place and the Ancient One sat down to judge. His clothing was as white as snow, his hair like purest wool. He sat on a fiery throne with wheels of blazing fire." Daniel 7:9.

DREAMS

White represents holiness, peace, the glory of God, and the righteousness of God. If you dream and see yourself dressed in white, it signifies that God has clothed you with His righteousness, which you cannot attain by your human efforts. It also denotes that the Lord is giving you His peace that is beyond all human understanding. However, if you are sick and see yourself dressed in white, pray against premature death.

Black: Death, Affliction, Deception, Adversity, Evil Persons

"Before I go to the place from which I shall not return, to the land of darkness and the shadow of death, a land as dark as darkness itself, as the shadow of death, without any order, where even the light is like darkness." Job 10:21-22. (NKJV)

The color black in dreams represents death, affliction, adversity, and evil. Sometimes it also represents the activities of evil people or the enemy around you. If someone in your dream appears dressed in black, it is a message from the Lord that the person, despite any good nature they may display outwardly to you, does not seek your good. They are evil.

If you also see in your dream something that is not meant to be naturally black become black, it signifies that affliction, adversity, or death is coming to that thing. Pray aggressively against calamity, death, and evil if you see this in your dream.

Blue - Knowledge, Word of God, Revelation, Heaven

If you see blue in your dream, it refers to knowledge, revelation, the word of God, and heaven. For example, if you see someone that you know or have heard of dressed in blue, it usually means that there is some knowledge or revelation that the person has that you need in your life. Get close to the person, either in person or through any resources they might have made available to learn from them. They hold valuable knowledge that you need.

Also, if you see a blue book or blue birds, it means that you need to seek knowledge.

However, if you see a blue sky, it could mean heaven.

Green - Life, Immortality, Flourishing, Restoration, Fertility, Prosperity, Fruitfulness

"For he shall be like a tree planted by the waters, which spreads out its roots by the river, and will not fear when heat comes; but its leaf will be green, and will not be anxious in the year of drought, nor will cease from yielding fruit." Jeremiah 17:8 (NKJV)

If you see green in your dream, it is a good dream. It means prosperity, a new life, flourishing, restoration, and fertility.

Are you currently barren but dreamed and saw yourself wearing green? Be excited. Your child is coming. Are you trying to start a business and noticed that the building was painted green? It is a sign from the Lord that the business will succeed. You can go ahead.

What if you saw brown leaves becoming green? It is a sign of restoration from the Lord.

Purple: Kingship, Royalty, Leadership, Honor, Wealth

"He made its pillars of silver, its support of gold, its seat of purple, its interior paved with love by the daughters of Jerusalem." Song of Solomon 3:10. (NKJV).

If you see purple in your dream, it signifies kingship, royalty, and leadership. Get ready to be promoted, elevated, and honored. God has bestowed honor upon you.

Gray: Wisdom, Maturity, Honor, Long Life, Humility, Repentance

"Gray hair is a crown of glory; it is gained by living a godly life." Proverbs 16:31.

If you see gray in your dream, it usually symbolizes wisdom, maturity, and honor. It could also mean a long life. The Bible usually associates gray hair with wisdom, maturity, honor, favor from God, and long life.

Gray can also mean the need to be humble and repent of something that displeases the Lord. Many times, in the Bible, kings of Israel who had disobeyed God would put on ashes and sackcloth as a sign of humility and repentance. Then the Lord, in turn, forgave and helped them.

Brown: Suffering, End of Season

"You will be like a great tree with withered leaves, like a garden without water. The strongest among you will disappear like straw; their evil deeds will be the spark that sets it on fire." Isaiah 1:30-31.

Brown represents suffering. A leaf could turn brown or wither if it is starved of nutrients, indicating suffering. The wooden cross of suffering that our Lord Jesus Christ carried was also brown.

Brown also means the end of a season. For example, in the fall season, leaves go from green to brown, marking the end of the summer season. Thus, seeing brown could represent the end of a season in your life. However, it could also mean that you would soon suffer if you do not make corrections.

Amber: Glory of God, Holiness

"Then I looked, and behold, a whirlwind was coming out of the north, a great cloud with raging fire engulfing itself; and brightness was all around it and

radiating out of its midst like the color of amber, out of the midst of the fire." Ezekiel 1:4. (NKJV)

If you see the color amber in your dream, it usually signifies the glory of God, the presence of God, and the holiness of God. If you are someone who has a heart for God and desire Him more than what He could give you, you may have this dream. If you also have a calling from God into a specific ministry in your life, you may also have this dream. It is an indication of God's special love for you. You are one of God's confidantes. Continue to engage in whatever you are doing that is pleasing to God, and you will experience a deeper dimension of Him.

CHAPTER 7

Animals In Dreams

Cow/Bull

Cows or bulls are common animals found worldwide. Many cultures consume them for their meat. In the case of cows, they are also milked for various human uses. However, in a dream, a cow or bull, especially a red or brown one usually does not indicate something good. It is often a representation of evil, sometimes a high-ranking evil person.

A Charging Cow/Bull

If in your dream you see a cow, bull, buffalo, moose, or any large animal charging at you, what does it mean?

Interpretation

It indicates that at least someone sees you as a threat and is already taking steps to eliminate you. If you are wounded in the dream, it could lead to death or a deadly injury that never heals in real life. But with God, victory is assured.

What To Do

- Do not panic.
- Start praising and worshipping God to take your focus off fear and stir up your faith.
- Pray warfare prayers.

Prayer Points

1. I take my position as a child of God and command that every weapon formed against me will not prosper (Isaiah 54:17).
2. My Father, in the name of Jesus, avenge me of everyone planning to eliminate me. *"And shall God not avenge His own elect who cry out day and night to Him, though He bears long with them? I tell you that He will avenge them speedily. Nevertheless, when the Son of Man comes, will He really find faith on the earth?" Luke 18:7-80. (NKJV)*
3. My Father, in the name of Jesus, heal me from every wound and injury, both known and unknown. *"Heal me, O LORD, and I shall be healed; Save me, and I shall be saved, For You are my praise." Jeremiah 17:14. (NKJV)*
4. In the name of Jesus, I declare that I will not die but live (Psalms 118:17).

A Cow/Bull Staring or Doing Nothing (Psalm 58:1-6)

You could also dream and see any large animal, such as those mentioned above, looking at you and doing nothing. It could also be following you around harmlessly. What does it mean?

Interpretation

If this was your dream, do not be deceived. It is still deadly. It means someone evil is around you. If the animal is in your house, someone close to you, in your circle, or maybe even living with you, is deadly. They appear harmless and trusting, but they are only waiting for a trigger to strike at your weakest moment.

What To Do

- Be careful who you tell your secrets to.
- Fast and pray.

Prayer Points

1. My Father, in the name of Jesus, as You exposed the sin of Achan in the Bible, expose everyone lying in wait to cause me harm (Joshua 7:18).
2. Holy Spirit of God, open my spiritual eyes, ears, and perceptions to know who not to relate with.
3. My Father, in the name of Jesus, according to Your word, let the evil planned for me return to the planner (Proverbs 26:27).

Killing A Cow/Bull

If you dream of killing a cow or bull, what could it mean?

Interpretation

It means victory over a high-ranking evil person. If you pray well, you should start to see changes in areas of your life that were once attacked by the enemy. It is possible for the person perpetrating this evil to suddenly become ill or expire.

What To Do

- Thank God for this victory.
- Pray for the manifestation of this dream.

Prayer Points

1. I use the sword of the Spirit to execute the demise of every symbolic cow or bull after my life in the name of Jesus (Ephesians 6:17).
2. My Father, in the name of Jesus, let my victory over unrepentant adversaries manifest physically now (Jeremiah 1:12).
3. Thank You, Father, for giving me victory over my unrepentant adversaries.

Lion

When you see a lion in your dream, what does it mean? In real life, a lion is the king of animals. It is not afraid of any animal or bird, no matter the size. It is courageous, strong, and fearless. A lion in a dream usually means something good. Our Lord Jesus is described as the Lion of the tribe of Judah (Revelation 5:5). A lion in a dream signifies our Lord Jesus, God's protection, and divine defense.

Lion Surrounding You or Your House

If you dream of a non-threatening lion or a pride of lions surrounding you or your house, what does it mean?

Interpretation

This signifies divine protection. The Lord is reassuring you of His divine protection around you, even though you may not see it with your physical eyes. The Bible tells us in Psalm 125:2, *"Just as the mountains surround Jerusalem, so the LORD surrounds his people, both now and forever."* If you are in a situation that terrifies you, the Lord is letting you know that you are not alone and are protected. The same applies if you see a lion roaring but not against you. It is to warn off would-be attackers.

What To Do

- Thank the Lord for protecting you.
- Pray for the protection of God not to leave you.
- Pray that your faith will be emboldened.

Prayer Points

1. Thank You, Father, for Your continuous protection around me.
2. Father, in the name of Jesus, do not let Your protection leave me.
3. Father, in the name of Jesus, do not let me do what would make Your presence leave me.
4. I receive a boldened faith in Jesus' name.

Lion Against You

What if you see a lion against you in your dream? If a lion roars at you, chases you, scares you, or bites you, what does it mean?

Interpretation

If a lion is against you in your dream, such as roaring, chasing, scaring, or biting you, it is not of God. It is the devil orchestrating the attacks of stubborn, determined, unyielding enemies against your life. He wants to eliminate you (1 Peter 5:8).

What To Do

- Thank the Lord that you were not eliminated.
- Be watchful and alert. *"Stay alert! Watch out for your great enemy, the devil. He prowls around like a roaring lion, looking for someone to devour." 1 Peter 5:8.*
- Resist the devil in prayers and stand strong in your faith. *"Stand firm against him, and be strong in your faith." 1 Peter 5:9.*

Prayer Points

1. Father, thank You that I was not consumed by my dream.
2. Father, in the name of Jesus, help me to be watchful and always alert.
3. In the name of Jesus, let the spirit of boldness and courage come upon me now.
4. In the name of Jesus, I put on the whole armor of God and come against every lion that is against me. I am executing judgment on you now.
5. In the name of Jesus, I come against every stubborn and unyielding pursuer of my life. Fall now (Isaiah 54:15).
6. In the name of Jesus, I command complete healing and total recovery from every attack of evil lions in my life now.

Snake

"He laid hold of the dragon, that serpent of old, who is the Devil and Satan, and bound him for a thousand years;" (Revelation 20:2).

One of the common animals that many people see in dreams are snakes. Whenever a snake appears in your dream, it is not good. It doesn't matter what the snake is doing in your dream; it never represents anything good. Snakes generally indicate witchcraft or the devil.

A Curling Snake

If you see a snake in a curling position, and not doing anything in your dream, is it harmless? What does it mean?

Interpretation

Seeing this dream doesn't mean the snake is harmless. God is telling you that someone around you is evil, a witch, or engaged in witchcraft. The curling position could indicate that the person is not yet showing their true colors to you. They are waiting for the perfect time to bare their fangs and afflict you.

What To Do

- Increase the tempo of prayer in your life and do not stop.
- Before bedtime, pray for at least 30 minutes.
- If you continue to see this dream, intensify your prayers to at least an hour and start from 11 PM or midnight.

Prayer Points

1. Father, in the name of Jesus, let Your fire give unrest to anyone with diabolical plans around me.
2. Father, in the name of Jesus, I am Your child. Clothe me with Your untouchable fire (Hebrews 12:29).

A Crawling Snake

If you notice a snake crawling in your dream, what does it mean?

Interpretation

It indicates that witchcraft is active in your life. It has penetrated a particular area of your life.

What To Do

- Think about your life. Where are you experiencing setbacks, failure, bad luck, or disappointment? That is where witchcraft is active.
- Beginning from 11 PM, every night for three nights, pray for at least two hours.

Prayer Points

1. In the name of Jesus, I rain the fire of God upon every witch and everyone practicing witchcraft around me.
2. It is written, *"He frustrates the devices of the crafty, so that their hands cannot carry out their plans." Job 5:12. (NKJV)* Therefore, I command in the name of Jesus that every work of witchcraft in my health, business, family, career, marriage, and finances be frustrated in Jesus' name.

Bitten By A Snake

If you were bitten by a snake in your dream, what does it mean?

Interpretation

This indicates a witchcraft attack on your health. It means satanic poison has been deposited into your system. Until this is out of your body, it may lead to chronic and terminal diseases, especially cancer. It could also lead to wounds that never heal.

What To Do

- Do not panic.
- Fast and pray for at least three days. Fast during the day and pray at least three times every day. In the morning and afternoon, pray for at least 30 minutes if possible. At night, pray from 11 PM or midnight for at least two hours.
- In the morning and afternoon, pray for at least 30 minutes if possible. At night, pray from 11 PM or midnight for at least two hours.
- After praying the prayers below, it is possible to start seeing yourself throwing up, going to the bathroom and emptying your bowels, or sweating profusely. You may increase the number of days of your prayers but not less than three days.

Prayer Points

1. "It is written, *'No weapon formed against you shall prosper...' Isaiah 54:17. (NKJV)* Therefore, Father, in the name of Jesus, immunize me from witchcraft attacks.
2. "It is written, *'He sent His word and healed them, and delivered them from their destructions.' Psalms 107:20. (NKJV)* Father, in the name of Jesus, heal me from the effects of every serpentine deposit in my body and deliver me from destruction.
3. Get a bottle of water. Pray into the water this way: "Let the healing and deliverance power of Jesus enter into this water. This water is no longer water but infused with the power of Jesus. As I drink it now, let it attack every serpentine poison in my system and set me free in Jesus' name."
4. I lift up Jesus and look up to Him. Therefore, the activity of witchcraft is powerless in my life. *"So Moses made a snake out of bronze and attached it to a pole. Then anyone who was bitten by a snake could look at the bronze snake and be healed!" Numbers 21:9.*

Snake Wrapped Around Your Legs or Hands

If a snake is wrapped around your legs or your hands, what does it mean?

Interpretation

This means an attack on your business, career, or profession. It could also extend to your finances, progress, dream, or vision. The goal of the enemy is to stagnate you or cause backwardness in your life. Progress may become very slow. You may also notice that what others obtain easily requires rigorous work and hard labor for you to get.

What To Do

- Do not panic.
- Shake it into the fire of God through prayer.

Prayer Points

1. Pray like this: In the name of Jesus, I shake every snake fastened around me into the fire of God. "As Paul gathered an armful of sticks and was laying them on the fire, a poisonous snake, driven out by the heat, bit him on the hand. But Paul shook off the snake into the fire and was unharmed." Acts 28:3-5.
2. In the name of Jesus, every chain of restriction tied around me, be broken off now.

Walking On Snakes

If you dreamed that you were walking on snakes, what does it mean?

Interpretation

It signifies that God has given you victory over the powers of darkness, especially witchcraft. Therefore, you should not be afraid. It is the same interpretation if you find yourself stepping on or driving over snakes.

DREAMS

What To Do

- Thank God for this dream.
- Pray for the manifestation of the dream. Remember that good dreams are not self-fulfilling. We must pray for their manifestation.

Prayer Points

1. Thank You, Father, for this dream.
2. In the name of Jesus, I trample upon and exercise my authority over snakes, scorpions, and all the power of the enemy at work in any area of my life (Luke 10:19).
3. In the name of Jesus, I enforce my complete victory over the work of evil in my life.
4. Let my victory become a reality now, in Jesus' name.

Monkey

Another common dream is about monkeys. If you see a monkey in your dream, what does it mean? First, look at the nature of monkeys generally. What do they do? They are crafty and cunning. They could pretend to be friendly for one minute, and the next minute they suddenly turn on you and steal from you. They could even harm you if you have something and refuse to give it to them.

Interpretation

If you see a monkey in your dream, God is telling you that someone close to you is tricky and cunning. Though they may appear to be friendly, they will soon turn against you. They are two-faced. They may flatter you, but it is for what they want to get from you. They are prepared to harm you for what you have if you don't give it to them. Someone who was like that in the Bible was Ahithophel. He was a confidante of David who turned on him when an opportunity presented itself during the rebellion of Absalom, David's son (2 Samuel 15-17).

What To Do

- Examine your life. Who are the people in your circle?
- Filter the level of access to you.
- Are you the most blessed, gifted, or sought after in your circle? It usually breeds envy.
- Pray.

Prayer Points

1. Father, in the name of Jesus, by Your Holy Spirit, expose all two-faced people in my life.
2. Father, in the name of Jesus, just like You did for David, defeat the plan of two-faced people in my life (2 Samuel 17:14).
3. Father, in the name of Jesus, just like Ahithophel, let crafty characters around me fall into their own trap (2 Samuel 17:13).
4. Father, in the name of Jesus, give me wisdom to deal with people.

Dog

Have you seen a dog in your dream? What do you think it means? I know this may break many hearts, especially dog lovers like me. Dogs are adorable, loyal, and faithful companions. Sadly, even though dogs are friendly in real life, they seem not to represent anything good in dreams.

Interpretation

In the Bible, dogs are associated with the sexually immoral (Revelation 22:15, Deuteronomy 23:18). If you see a friendly dog around you in your dream, it usually indicates that the spirit of sexual immorality is at work in your life or has polluted your life. If you don't urgently address it, it will

DREAMS

open the door for the devil to have access to legally oppress and torment you.

What To Do

- ▸ The first step is to confess your sins to God and ask Him for forgiveness.
- ▸ Cast out the unclean spirit from your life.
- ▸ Confess Jesus as the Lord of your life.
- ▸ Completely surrender your life to Jesus.

Prayer Points

1. Father, in the name of Jesus, please forgive me for the sin of _____. Cleanse me by the blood of Jesus.
2. Put one hand on your head and pray this way: "As I begin to pray now, I confess that my entire body is the temple of the Holy Spirit. Therefore, every spirit of lust, immorality, pornography, fornication, and adultery or any other unclean spirit not mentioned at work in my life, get out in Jesus' name."
3. As you begin to pray this prayer, touch every part of your body (e.g., eyes, ears, hands). Pray like this: "In the name of Jesus, whatever medium spirit of lust, immorality, pornography, fornication, or adultery may have entered into my life, exit now never to return in Jesus' name."
4. "I confess that Jesus is the Lord of my life. He is the Lord over my spirit, soul, and body. I give my life completely to You, Jesus, and submit to You. Therefore, exercise Your Lordship over my life. Take over."

Dogs Barking at You

If you see a dog barking at you in your dream, what does it mean?

Interpretation

This means that the enemy is aggressively working hard to prevent you from accomplishing some definite goals you are currently aiming for. He wants to put fear into you so you can abandon your goals. He knows that if you are left alone, you can attain your goals. This is usually the work of witchcraft.

What To Do

- Determine to be strong in the Lord by reading the Scriptures.
- Pray aggressively, especially at night.

Prayer Points

1. In the name of Jesus, I put on the whole armor of God (Ephesians 6:10-18).
2. In the name of Jesus, I come against every power resisting my progress and advancement. I render you powerless now.
3. In the name of Jesus, I destroy the work of witchcraft in my life (Job 5:13).
4. In the name of Jesus, I bind every witch operating against me. No more (Matthew 18:18).
5. In the name of Jesus, I silence permanently every symbolic dog in my dream, never to appear anymore.

DREAMS

Bitten By a Dog

If you dream that a dog bites you, what does it mean? It is not good.

Interpretation

If a dog bites you in your dream, it speaks of a demonic deposit in your life. It is the work of witchcraft. Usually, this would be from someone who knows you. They may appear as friends, but they are not.

What To Do

- Muster courage.
- When you wake up, go into aggressive prayers.

Prayer Points

1. In the name of Jesus, I command every demonic deposit in my body to be neutralized now (Luke 10:19).
2. In the name of Jesus, I come against every power resisting my progress and advancement. I render you powerless now.
3. In the name of Jesus, I destroy every work of witchcraft in my life (Job 5:13).
4. In the name of Jesus, I come against every coven operating against me. Be consumed by the fire of God (Hebrews 12:29).
5. In the name of Jesus, I silence permanently every symbolic dog in my dream, never to appear again.

Rats/Mice

Another common dream involves rats or mice. What do rats, mice, or any rodents mean in your dream? Remember that to interpret your dream, you don't need to have this exact dream. You just need to examine the similarities, the main characters, objects, or events.

Interpretation

What are the characteristics of rats/mice? They eat or devour just about anything. They are associated with dirty places and scavenging from trash. They are irritable to most people. Rats, mice, or rodents of any kind or color in a dream are never symbols of anything good.

1. **Devourer**: A rat in your dream symbolizes a devourer. It could be a devourer in your finances, health, career, etc. Unless you do something about it, anything you touch or do would amount to nothing. If it's your health, you'd be suffering from one health crisis after another.
2. **Chronic or Generational Poverty:** Rats or rodents of any kind could also mean that the spirit of generational poverty is at work in your life.

What To Do

- One of the things that trigger devourers is disobedience to God. Check your life to see if you are disobedient to God in any of His instructions to you and make amends (Haggai 1:5-11, Malachi 3:8-12).
- Examine your family. Is there a pattern of poverty? Do all it takes for it to end with you.
- Pray aggressively for three nights or until the dream stops and changes begin.

Prayer Points

1. Father, in the name of Jesus, forgive me wherever I have disobeyed You and have mercy on me.
2. Father, in the name of Jesus, I promise to obey You completely. I rebuke devourers in my life (Malachi 3:11).

3. In the name of Jesus, I break the stronghold of the strongman of generational poverty over my life (Mark 3:27-29).
4. I terminate, by the blood of Jesus, every inherited legal hold of poverty over my life.
5. Jesus, I exchange my poverty for riches now. Let it become a reality in my life (2 Corinthians 8:9).

Killing A Rat or Mice

If you see in your dream that you killed a rat, mice, or any rodent, what could it mean?

Interpretation

If this was your dream, rejoice. The Lord is telling you that you have victory over devourers. It is also a sign that you have victory over the spirit of poverty.

What To Do

- Give thanks to God for your victory.
- Start praying that the dream becomes a reality.

Prayer Points

1. Father, in the name of Jesus, thank You for giving me victory over the devourer and poverty.
2. In the name of Jesus, I decree victory over every activity of the devourer in my life.
3. In the name of Jesus, I enforce my victory over the spirit of poverty permanently (2 Corinthians 8:9).
4. In the name of Jesus, I command every spiritual hindrance to the manifestation of this victory to be removed (Daniel 10:13).

CHAPTER 8

Birds In Dreams

Birds

Birds also have meanings in dreams. There are many birds with different meanings, but we'll focus on a few commonly seen in dreams. When interpreting a bird in a dream, you can generally consider its character or nature to understand the message being conveyed. The guidelines below generally apply to all birds in dreams, with very few exceptions:

Singing Bird

If you dream and see a bird singing, expect good news.

Bird Sitting On Eggs In A Nest

If you see a bird sitting on eggs in a nest in your dream, it means you should work hard on your ideas and be persistent. This will produce good results, including in your career or profession.

Dead Bird Falling From The Sky

If you see a dead bird falling from the sky in your dream, it indicates that bad news or disappointment is approaching.

Surrounded By Beautiful Birds

If you see yourself surrounded by beautiful birds in your dream, it signifies success, goodness, celebration, and prosperity coming your way.

Eggs In A Nest

If you see intact eggs in a nest in your dream, it means you will have financial success and experience good fortunes.

Duck

I have met folks who have dreamed of seeing ducks. Have you seen a duck in your dream, maybe swimming? What might that signify?

Interpretation

Ducks are aquatic birds found in lakes, ponds, rivers, etc. But they can also walk on land and fly. If you see a duck swimming in a body of water, it signifies success in your endeavors. A duck's webbed feet allow it to swim, float, catch food efficiently, and navigate quickly, helping it evade predators and migrate effectively.

If you see a duck swimming in your dream, it means that even though the task before you may look fearful or dangerous (water), do not be afraid. You have been equipped for it by the Lord. It also means the enemy's attack will not touch you. You will not sink. You will easily navigate your way.

What To Do

1. Thank God for this dream.
2. Step out in faith with tasks before you and don't be afraid.
3. Pray that God will prosper all your endeavors.

Prayer Points

1. Father, thank You for this dream.
2. Father, in the name of Jesus, give me the grace to step out in faith and not be afraid (Numbers 14:24).
3. Father, in the name of Jesus, prosper all my endeavors (Psalm 1:3).
4. Father, in the name of Jesus, let this dream become a reality as You have revealed it to me (Acts 27:25).
5. Father, in the name of Jesus, give me victory always. Don't let me sink in the problems of life (1 John 5:4).

Bat

If you see a bat in your dream, what does it mean?

Interpretation

Along with snakes, bats are one of the preferred creatures used by the kingdom of darkness to signal and cause evil. In Leviticus 11:19, bats are listed as detestable creatures. Seeing one in your dream indicates the presence of a demonic agent in your life. It means something bad is bound to happen unless you resist it through prayers. Bats can also cause afflictions, especially if bitten by one in a dream. They can be used to attack your financial fortunes.

What To Do

- ▸ Create an atmosphere that is inconducive for demonic agents around you through praise and worship.
- ▸ Put on the whole armor of God.
- ▸ Develop the habit of praying at night.
- ▸ Pray.

Prayer Points

1. Father, I praise You because You are the Almighty God.
2. In the name of Jesus, I intercept and void every attack on my finances.
3. In the name of Jesus, I destroy every instrument of affliction deployed against me.
4. Father, in the name of Jesus, let Your holy presence continually surround me (Psalm 125:2).

Chicken

If you see a chicken in your dream, what does it mean?

Interpretation

Seeing a chicken in your dream signifies fear and cowardice. It means you are afraid and lack boldness, courage, and confidence. Before you can move forward and make remarkable progress in your life, you need to address this fear. This fear may not be just physical but spiritual as well. It could be the spirit of fear at work in you.

What To Do

- ▸ Are you fond of procrastination? Could it be because of fear?
- ▸ Examine yourself. When was the last time you took a daring step?

DREAMS

- Check. Do you suddenly become afraid when it's time to go after what you wanted?
- Pray.

Prayer Points

1. In the name of Jesus, I come against the spirit of fear. Get out of my life.
2. In the name of Jesus, I receive the spirit of power, love, and a sound mind. *"For God has not given us a spirit of fear, but of power and of love and of a sound mind." 2 Timothy 1:7. (NKJV)*
3. I declare in the name of Jesus that I am strong in the Lord.
4. I declare in the name of Jesus that I am strong in the power of His might.
5. I command the spirit of courage and boldness to rise within me now.

Ostrich Walking Around

If you saw an ostrich strutting majestically in your dream, what does it mean?

Interpretation

The ostrich is the tallest of all birds with no equal in height. This indicates a leadership role opening up for you. It could also mean that you will rise and excel in whatever you are currently doing, even if you have not been equipped like others.

What To Do

- Start to prepare yourself for leadership.
- Be careful of character flaws that could disqualify you (Hebrews 1:9).

- Pray for it to happen.

Prayer Points

1. Father, in the name of Jesus, help me to hate sin and love righteousness (Hebrews 1:9).
2. Father, in the name of Jesus, lift up my head above my contemporaries (Psalm 3:3).
3. In the name of Jesus, I come against every attempt to bring me down.

Ostrich With Head Buried In The Sand

If what you saw is an ostrich with its head buried in the sand, it has a different meaning.

Interpretation

It means that you live a carefree life and can care less about what happens around you. It could also mean that you are stubbornly set in your ways.

What To Do

- Examine your life. Are you living a carefree life?
- Start making amends.
- Pray against foolishness.

Prayer Points

1. Father, in the name of Jesus, show me where I live carelessly.
2. In the name of Jesus, I will not be a fool.
3. In the name of Jesus, I will not suffer like a fool (2 Samuel 3:33).

Dove

One of the common birds that people dream of is a dove. If you see a dove in your dream, what does it mean?

Interpretation

This is a common interpretation. It is a good dream. A dove symbolizes the presence of the Holy Spirit, indicating that the Holy Spirit is around you.

What To Do

- Give thanks to God for His presence.
- Pray that the abiding presence of the Holy Spirit will not leave you.

Prayer Points

1. Thank You, Father, for the presence of Your Holy Spirit.
2. Father, in the name of Jesus, let the abiding presence of Your Spirit never leave me (Psalm 51:11).

Dove On Your Head

If you dream and see a dove landing on your head, what does it mean?

Interpretation

It indicates the empowerment (anointing) of the Holy Spirit in your life. The Bible tells us that when Jesus was baptized, the Holy Spirit descended from heaven in the form of a dove on Jesus' head. So, a dove on your head means that the Holy Spirit is empowering you for a ministry or tasks that He has for you, and He wants you to be aware of this (Acts 1:8, Luke 3:22-24). It could also indicate that a new gift of the Holy Spirit has been given to you (I Corinthians 12:7-11).

What To Do

- ▸ Give thanks to God for His anointing on your life.
- ▸ Begin to walk in this new awareness.
- ▸ Pray to fan into flames this empowerment (I Timothy 1:18).

Prayer Points

1. Father, thank You for anointing me.
2. In the name of Jesus, I begin to walk and work in this new level of anointing.
3. In the name of Jesus, let this anointing manifest physically in my life.
4. In the name of Jesus, I overcome challenges with this new anointing.

Owl

If you dream and see an owl, what does it mean? Or if you constantly see an owl in real life, what does it mean?

Interpretation

If you see an owl in your dream, it signifies that evil agents are watching and monitoring you. They watch and monitor every move you make. In the spirit realm, it is possible to observe what a person is doing without being physically present. The result of this could be failure, stagnation, sickness, and even death. A popular young actor on TV shared that he constantly saw an owl in every city he visited. Unfortunately, he received the wrong interpretation of what it meant, and it didn't end well.

What To Do

- ▸ Do not panic if you see this in your dream or in real life.
- ▸ Remember that you are valuable, which is why evil agents are watching you.
- ▸ Stand strong in faith.
- ▸ Pray aggressive prayers.

DREAMS

Prayer Points

1. Father, thank You that You are always with me.
2. In the name of Jesus, I command the eyes of every evil agent monitoring me to be blinded by the power of God (Genesis 19:11).
3. In the name of Jesus, anytime my name is summoned in the occult world, let the blood of Jesus answer (Revelation 12:11).
4. It is written, *"Behold, the eye of the LORD is on those who fear Him..." Psalm 33:18. (NKJV)* Therefore, every harm planned for me is voided in Jesus' name.
5. It is written, *"...when the enemy comes in like a flood, the Spirit of the Lord will lift up a standard against him." Isaiah 59:19. (NKJV)* Therefore, Spirit of the Lord, raise up a standard against every enemy coming against me.

Eagle

Interpretation

Seeing an eagle in your dream generally means that you will go through a turbulent time. However, God has equipped you to soar above it, especially if you wait on Him in prayers (Isaiah 40:31). It could also mean that the Lord has anointed you with the gift of a prophet (I Corinthians 12:10). You will be able to see the invisible and hear the inaudible. God has chosen you.

What To Do

- Examine your life and observe how this applies to you.
- Pray for this empowerment to manifest in your life.

Prayer Points

1. Father, thank You for this dream.
2. In the name of Jesus, let this empowerment become a reality in my life.

3. Father, in the name of Jesus, I wait on You. Renew my strength (Isaiah 40:31).
4. In the name of Jesus, I soar like eagles over every turbulent situation in my life.
5. In the name of Jesus, my spiritual eyes are open to see the invisible. My spiritual ears are open to hear the inaudible (I Kings 6:17).

Pigeon

If you see a pigeon in your dream, what does it mean?

Interpretation

A pigeon symbolizes peace, freedom, and prosperity. It could also indicate that good news is on the horizon. However, if you scare away the pigeon, it means you may have a bad attitude that repels people.

What To Do

- Pray that the good dream manifests.
- If you scared away the pigeon, watch your attitude. Develop a friendly demeanor.

Prayer Points

1. Father, in the name of Jesus, let Your good dream for me become a reality.
2. In the name of Jesus, let peace, freedom, and prosperity become a reality in my life now.
3. In the name of Jesus, I will not repel my divine helpers (Proverbs 18:24).

CHAPTER 9

Fruits In Dreams

"The fruit of the righteous is a tree of life..." Proverbs 11:30. NKJV

Fruits in dreams have meanings. Depending on the fruit you see, it could tell you about what you are going through or what is to come. However, the condition and the location of the fruit in your dream matter.

Ripened Fruit

If you see a ripened fruit in your dream, what does it mean?

Interpretation

A ripened fruit in your dream is usually a good dream. It means you have a blessing coming to you from the Lord. Your blessing is ready. It is near you. It is within reach and should manifest any moment from now.

What To Do

- Thank God for showing this dream to you.
- Pray aggressively that your blessing will not be sabotaged, rerouted, or delayed.
- Pray aggressively for the manifestation of your dream because good things attract the enemy's attention for sabotage.

Prayer Points

1. Father, thank You for preparing a blessing for me.
2. Father, in the name of Jesus, protect the blessing You have prepared for me from sabotage, detour, or delay.
3. In the name of Jesus, every weapon launched against my blessing has become useless now.
4. Father, in the name of Jesus, let the blessing You have prepared for me manifest now (Ezekiel 12:23).
5. I command the heavenlies to be cleared for the prompt arrival of my blessing in Jesus' name (Daniel 10:21).

Unripe Fruit

If you see an unripe fruit in your dream, what does it mean?

Interpretation

"This vision is for a future time. It describes the end, and it will be fulfilled. If it seems slow in coming, wait patiently, for it will surely take place. It will not be delayed." Habakkuk 2:3.

If you see unripe fruit in your dream, it means your answer or blessing is in progress. It is loading. If you find yourself plucking an unripe fruit, it means you are impatient. You should patiently wait on the Lord for the appropriate time.

DREAMS

What To Do:

- ▸ Thank God for showing this dream to you.
- ▸ Pray for the grace to wait on the Lord.
- ▸ Pray aggressively that the work the Lord started in your life will not be stalled.
- ▸ Pray that the Lord will hide your blessing until the day of manifestation.
- ▸ Pray that the Lord will hasten the performance of this blessing.

Prayer Points

1. Father, thank You for preparing a blessing for me.
2. In the name of Jesus, my blessing won't be delayed or aborted.
3. Father, in the name of Jesus, do not let the work You have started in my life be stalled (Philippians 1:6).
4. Father, in the name of Jesus, hide my blessing until the day of manifestation (Luke 1:80).
5. Father, hasten the performance of this blessing now (Jeremiah 1:12).
6. In the name of Jesus, I receive the grace to wait on the Lord.

Bad or Rotten Fruit

If you see a rotten or bad fruit in your dream, what does it mean?

Interpretation

A rotten or bad fruit in your dream means your blessing has been corrupted or sabotaged. It could also mean that you have wasted your blessings due to pride or ignorance.

What To Do

- ▸ Thank God for showing this dream to you.
- ▸ Pray aggressively against forces that corrupt blessings.

- Ask for God's mercy in any way you might have wasted your blessings.
- Ask God for forgiveness for the spirit of pride if applicable.

Prayer Points

1. Father, thank You for showing this dream to me.
2. Father, I ask for Your mercy in any way I might have ignorantly or carelessly wasted my blessings (Romans 9:15).
3. Father, forgive me for any trace of the spirit of pride in my life in Jesus' name (1 John 1:9).
4. Father, redeem and restore my life in Jesus' name (Psalm 107:2).

Fruit On A Tree

If you see a fruit or fruits on a tree in your dream, what does it mean?

Interpretation

A fruit or fruits on a tree in your dream while you are on the ground means your blessing or answer is beyond your reach. It could mean that you are being prevented spiritually from reaching your blessing. It could also mean that the enemy wants you to struggle, engage in hard labor before you obtain your blessing.

What To Do

- Thank God for showing this dream to you.
- Pray aggressively against forces that are making your blessings beyond your reach.
- Pray aggressively against forces of hard labor.
- Ask for God's mercy.

Prayer Points

1. Father, thank You for showing this dream to me.
2. Father, I ask for Your mercy. Be merciful to me (Romans 9:15).
3. In the name of Jesus, I bind forces making my blessings beyond my reach (Matthew 18:18).
4. In the name of Jesus, I break every hold of hard labor over my life.

Apple

If you see an apple in your dream, what does it mean?

Interpretation

"Keep me as the apple of your eye; hide me in the shadow of your wings." Psalm 17:8. (NKJV)

An apple, like many fruits you see in your dreams, signifies fruitfulness. It also means abundance and prosperity. Additionally, seeing an apple could indicate that, despite what you are going through, you are very special to the Lord (Psalm 17:8). On the other hand, an apple could also signify temptation—a warning that the devil is attempting to lure you with lust or greed.

What To Do

- Thank God for this dream.
- Assess it in the context of what is going on in your life.
- If you are in a tough situation, rejoice because God is still with you, just like He was with Joseph in prison.
- Be watchful of temptation to lure you.

Prayer Points

1. Father, thank You for this dream.

2. Father, in the name of Jesus, let it be seen physically that I am special to You (Psalm 17:8).
  3. Father, in the name of Jesus, show me the favor You give to those who wait on You (Isaiah 30:18).
  4. Father, in the name of Jesus, show me the way of escape out of every temptation (1 Corinthians 10:13).
  5. Father, in the name of Jesus, reveal to me any weakness that I may have.

Grapes

If you see grapes in your dream, what do they mean?

Interpretation

"Your threshing season will overlap with the grape harvest, and your grape harvest will overlap with the season of planting grain. You will eat your fill and live securely in your own land." Leviticus 26:5.

If you see grapes in your dream, it signifies fruitfulness, success in life, a good life, sweetness, celebration, and God's blessings. It also means fertility.

What To Do

- Thank God for the dream.
- Pray to God for the manifestation of all the good things this dream represents in your life.
- Pray to God that you will not do anything that would disqualify you from this blessing.

Prayer Points

  1. Thank You, Lord, for remembering me.
  2. Father, in the name of Jesus, hasten this good dream to becoming a reality now (Habakkuk 2:3).

3. In the name of Jesus, I take charge of the spiritual atmosphere of my life. I clear the spiritual highways for my blessings to manifest unhindered in Jesus' name (Daniel 10:13).
4. In the name of Jesus, I declare that I begin to enjoy success in life, a good life, sweetness, celebration, and God's blessings in Jesus' name (Proverbs 18:21).
5. In the name of Jesus, I will not do anything that would disqualify me from this blessing.

Orange

If you see an orange fruit in your dream, what does it mean?

Interpretation

Orange is a universal fruit found almost everywhere in the world. Dreaming of an orange indicates a reward for your labor. It means prosperity, abundance, and financial success. Its vibrant color signifies joy and happiness for you. When you bite into and savor the juice of a ripe orange, you feel nourished and content. Dreaming of an orange fruit signifies contentment and satisfaction ahead for you.

What To Do

- ▸ Thank God for this dream.
- ▸ If you are in a tough situation, cheer up because your joy is around.
- ▸ Pray for the manifestation of the dream for at least three nights.

Prayer Points

1. Father, thank You for this dream.
2. In the name of Jesus, let there be the physical manifestation of this dream now.

3. In the name of Jesus, let the plans of the enemy against this dream be voided now (Job 5:12).
4. Father, in the name of Jesus, hasten the manifestation of this dream now (Jeremiah 1:12).
5. In the name of Jesus, I will not die before, during, and after the manifestation of this dream.

Squeezed Orange

If the orange you see in your dream is being squeezed or juiced, what does it mean?

Interpretation

"You have planted much but harvest little. You eat but are not satisfied. You drink but are still thirsty. You put on clothes but cannot keep warm. Your wages disappear as though you were putting them in pockets filled with holes!" Haggai 1:6.

If the orange you saw in your dream is being squeezed or juiced by someone else, it signifies exploitation or being drained. It could also signify the enemy's attack on your blessings, where the enemy is consuming the reward of your labor. Not obeying the Lord gives the enemy the legal right to attack your blessings.

What To Do

- Do a thorough self-assessment of current happenings in your life.
- Let go of things that are injurious to your peace and health.
- Pray against the attack of the devil on your blessings.
- Ask the Lord to rebuke the devourer in your life.
- Pray the prayers below for at least three nights.

DREAMS

Prayer Points

1. Father, thank You for Your love for me.
2. Father, in the name of Jesus, forgive me for any disobedience that has given the enemy legal rights into my life. Have mercy on me.
3. Father, in the name of Jesus, rebuke the devourer of my blessings (Malachi 3:11).
4. In the name of Jesus, I frustrate every attack of the enemy on my blessings now (Luke 10:19).
5. In the name of Jesus, every stronghold of the thief over my blessings be broken now (John 10:10).

Pineapple

If you see pineapple in your dream, what does it mean?

Interpretation

Pineapple has a rough external appearance, but the inside is sweet, succulent, and nourishing. Dreaming of a pineapple signifies sweetness, blessings, and good things coming your way despite any opposition. If you are working on a project or have started something that appears thorny or difficult, don't give up. Your effort will be worth it.

What To Do

- Thank God for this encouragement.
- Be strong and feed your faith with scriptures and motivational content.
- Pray for the manifestation.

Prayer Points

1. Father, thank You for this dream.
2. In the name of Jesus, I receive strength to persist.

3. Father, in the name of Jesus, fill me with the spirit of faith (2 Corinthians 4:13).
4. In the name of Jesus, let every opposition surrounding my goodness give way now.
5. In the name of Jesus, I will not die before my goodness manifests.
6. In the name of Jesus, I will not contract a terminal disease.

Palm Tree

If you see a palm tree in your dream, what does it mean?

Interpretation: *"The righteous shall flourish like a palm tree..." Psalms 92:12. (NKJV)*

The palm tree is well written about in the Bible. It is always associated with something good. The righteous are compared to a palm tree in Psalms 92:12. The palm tree has many uses, such as providing coconut, dates, palm oil (outer layer), palm kernel oil (inner seed), palm fronds (leaves) for thatch roofs, baskets, and brooms (leaves), fuel (oil & leaves), construction (leaves), insulation (leaves), and wax (oil). So, it could signify that God has given you talents and abilities that will yield blessings in many ways. This would make you flourish. Also, the palm tree grows very tall, taller than many trees. This signifies a long life for you.

What To Do

- Give thanks to God for this dream.
- Do an inventory of your talents, skills, and abilities. Are you maximizing them? What have you discovered?
- Be a continuous blessing to others.
- Pray that the Lord will protect you from the attack of the evil one.
- Pray against powers frustrating your abilities to turn your dreams into physical blessings.
- Pray that long life will become a reality for you.

Prayer Points

1. Father, thank You for this dream.
2. Father, in the name of Jesus, protect me from the attack of the evil one (Matthew 6:13).
3. Father, in the name of Jesus, let those who need my skills and abilities and would pay a premium for them locate me now (Proverbs 18:16).
4. Father, in the name of Jesus, connect me with those who have what I need now (Genesis 41:12).
5. In the name of Jesus, I frustrate every power frustrating my efforts and abilities now.
6. Father, in the name of Jesus, satisfy me with long life (Psalms 91:16).

CHAPTER 10

Food & Drinks in Dreams

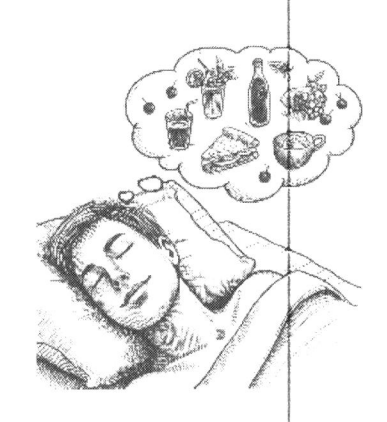

Eating or Drinking In Your Dream

"A hungry person dreams of eating but wakes up still hungry. A thirsty person dreams of drinking but is still faint from thirst when morning comes..." Isaiah 29:8.

Eating or drinking in a dream is quite common and can happen for various reasons. You might have been hungry or thirsty before bed, or it could be due to demonic manipulation.

Interpretation

While sometimes harmless, eating or drinking in a dream can also be sinister. Satanic agents might feed you poisonous food or drink that appears normal due to witchcraft manipulations. These substances, though they may seem harmless or even delicious, can introduce deadly diseases like cancer, infertility, or chronic illnesses. Consuming food in a dream can also be a method for demonic control through witchcraft.

What To Do

- If you eat in your dream, avoid eating or drinking anything until after 12 noon the next day.
- If you must eat or drink before then, pray the following prayers first.

Prayer Points

1. It is written, *"...and if they drink anything deadly, it will by no means hurt them..." Mark 16:18. (NKJV)* Therefore, in the name of Jesus, I neutralize any harmful effects of what I might have eaten or drunk in my dream.
2. It is written, *"No weapon formed against you shall prosper..." Isaiah 54:17. NKJV* Therefore, Father, in the name of Jesus, protect me from food and drink attacks.
3. It is written, *"So you shall serve the LORD your God, and He will bless your bread and your water. And I will take sickness away from the midst of you." Exodus 23:25.* Therefore, Father, in the name of Jesus, remove sickness from my body.
4. Open a bottle of water or a cup and pray over it: "Let this water become the blood of Jesus. As I drink it, let it neutralize any poisonous deposits in my system and render them ineffective."

Bread

Bread often appears in dreams. If you dream of seeing bread, whether a loaf or slices, here's what it might mean:

Interpretation

Bread symbolizes sustenance and can have several meanings:

- ▸ Your source of income, sustaining your family (Matthew 6:11).
- ▸ Food.
- ▸ The economy of a nation (Romans 1:6).
- ▸ The word of God, potentially indicating a calling into ministry.

What To Do

- ▸ Apply the dream within the context of your life.

Prayer Points

1. Father, in the name of Jesus, help me understand what I need to do with this dream.

Not Enough Bread

If you dream of not having enough bread, here's what it might mean:

Interpretation

- ▸ You may need to gain more knowledge and skills, especially if the bread was in a blue wrapper.
- ▸ Stay committed to what you're doing. Don't give up. Give thanks to God and continue your work. God will bless the work of your hands. Remember, Jesus used five loaves of bread and two fish to feed over 5,000 people, with leftovers (Matthew 14:13-21).
- ▸ If the dream shows widespread bread scarcity, it could mean the economy of your community or nation is going to decline.

What To Do

- Assess your source of income or skills. Identify your strengths and weaknesses and areas for improvement.
- Pray for God's blessings on your income.
- If there is widespread scarcity, ask God if you should relocate and where to go. Elisha told a woman to relocate due to an impending famine revealed by the Lord (2 Kings 8:1).

Prayer Points

1. Father, in the name of Jesus, bless the work of my hands and multiply my income (Psalm 138:8).
2. Father, in the name of Jesus, exempt me from scarcity. Show me where to go and what to do (2 Kings 8:1).

Feeding Others With Bread

If you dream of feeding others with bread, it could mean:

Interpretation

- God has called you to be a provider, a blessing, and a major helper to others.
- You might be called into ministry, especially as a teacher, pastor, or leader.

What To Do

- If you have a desire to help others, start doing so, even with little resources.
- If you feel a calling to serve God in ministry, this dream could confirm your calling.

Prayer Points

1. Father, in the name of Jesus, bless me so I can bless others (Genesis 12:2).
2. Father, in the name of Jesus, I surrender my life to You. Show me my purpose in life (Acts 13:22).

Eating Bread

If you find yourself eating bread in the dream, what does it mean?

Interpretation

This is one of those dreams where the context of what is currently going on in your life really matters.

- ▶ It might indicate that God is about to bless you. If you're going through a tough time, this dream could be a sign that a period of plenty and satisfaction is on its way (Ruth 1:6).
- ▶ It could also suggest that you are not managing your finances well. You might be spending everything without saving or planning for the future.

What To Do

- ▶ Objectively evaluate your life to see which scenario fits your situation.
- ▶ Act according to the relevant interpretation.

Prayer Points

1. Father, in the name of Jesus, visit me with Your blessings as You have promised (Ruth 1:6).
2. In the name of Jesus, let the blessings the Father has promised me become a reality with no hindrances (Jeremiah 1:12).

3. Father, in the name of Jesus, give me the power to overcome destructive spending habits.
4. In the name of Jesus, I will be a seed sower, planning for my future (2 Corinthians 9:10).

Cake

Have you seen a cake in your dream? Cakes are often associated with celebrations and joy in real life.

Seeing a Fully Made Cake, Eating, or Cutting a Cake

If you see a fully made cake, or you're eating or cutting a cake in your dream, it symbolizes upcoming celebrations. It means God has prepared a blessing for you that will bring joy and sweetness into your life. It could also indicate the successful completion of a task. However, it's important not to relax your efforts just yet.

What To Do

- Rejoice and give thanks to God.
- Keep up your current efforts.
- Believe that this celebration will come to pass.
- Pray for the manifestation of this blessing.
- Pray for good health to enjoy what God has planned for you.

Prayer Points

1. Father, thank You for remembering me.
2. It is written, *"the voice of rejoicing and salvation in the tents of the righteous..." Psalm 118:15. (NKJV)* Therefore, I declare this dream will become reality without delay in Jesus' name.
3. In the name of Jesus, I protect this dream and its manifestation from spiritual hijackers.

4. In the name of Jesus, I summon angelic reinforcement for the manifestation of this dream now (Daniel 10:21).
   5. In the name of Jesus, I will not die or be incapacitated before, during, and after the completion of the good things God has planned for me.

Half-Made Cake

How about seeing a half-made cake in your dream? What does this mean?

Interpretation

Seeing a half-made cake in your dream signifies something incomplete. It could mean that God has begun sending something good your way, but it's not yet finished. The dream encourages you to stay excited about what's coming and not to relax your efforts.

What To Do

- Give thanks to God for starting this work.
- Pray that what God has started will be completed without being hijacked.
- Pray for good health to enjoy what God has planned for you.
- Reflect on any areas where you might be tempted to relax your efforts.

Prayer Points

   1. Father, thank You for working on my matter.
   2. It is written, "being confident of this, that he who began a good work in you will carry it on to completion until the day of Christ Jesus." (Philippians 1:6 NIV). Therefore, in the name of Jesus, I decree that every good work God began in, for, and through me will not be hijacked, delayed, or disrupted.

3. In the name of Jesus, I will not die or be incapacitated before, during, and after the completion of the good work God has begun for me.

Ingredients For Making Cake

What if you see ingredients for making a cake but not a ready-made cake in your dream? What does it mean?

Interpretation

If you dream of seeing ingredients for making a cake but not a ready-made cake, it means God has given you the resources needed for a blessing. You must put in the effort to bring everything together and create the blessing you seek.

What To Do

- Reflect and read up on the blessing you seek for better understanding.
- Consider possible actions to take.
- Pray for wisdom and understanding.

Prayer Points

1. Father, thank You for giving me what I need.
2. Father, in the name of Jesus, give me the understanding of how to use what You have given me.
3. Father, in the name of Jesus, help me connect the dots and make sense of what I have.

Cake Stolen, Taken Away or Destroyed

What if you see that your cake was stolen, taken away, or destroyed?

Interpretation

If you dream that your cake was stolen, taken away, or destroyed, it signifies an interference with something good destined for you. It means a major setback at the edge of success, where promising endeavors suddenly halt.

What To Do

- Do not be afraid.
- Confront the enemy with aggressive prayers to reverse this dream.
- Pray and fast for at least three nights if what you are expecting is significant.

Prayer Points

1. Father, thank You for always being with me.
2. In the name of Jesus, I reverse this dream now.
3. In the name of Jesus, I cancel every plan to steal, take away, or destroy my celebration.
4. In the name of Jesus, I stand against every activity of symbolic snakes and scorpions in my life (Luke 10:19). Be destroyed now.
5. In the name of Jesus, I render every bewitchment, spell, or jinx aimed at causing a breakdown at the edge of success powerless now (Job 5:13).
6. Father, in the name of Jesus, as You restored the fortunes of Job, restore all my fortunes that have been stolen, taken away, or destroyed now (Job 42:10).

Milk & Honey

If you see milk or honey in your dream, what does it mean?

Interpretation

Dreaming of carrying milk or honey signifies that God has a plan to prosper you and bless the work of your hands. Just as God promised the Israelites a land flowing with milk and honey, this dream is a reassurance from God not to give up, even when times are tough. It indicates that better things are ahead.

What To Do

- Give thanks to God.
- Pray for the manifestation of this blessing, as good dreams often face opposition.

Prayer Points

1. Father, thank You for Your plan for me.
2. In the name of Jesus, let my prosperity manifest physically now (Ezekiel 12:23).
3. Father, in the name of Jesus, prosper the work of my hands (Psalm 138:8).
4. Father, in the name of Jesus, help me to be patient to receive my promise (Hebrews 10:35-36).

Someone After Your Milk or Honey

What if a cow, an animal, or a person is chasing you while you have milk or honey in your hand?

Interpretation

This dream means there are evil forces trying to hinder God's plan to prosper you. You need to wage spiritual warfare against them.

What To Do

- Engage in spiritual warfare against these forces.
- Take your stand as a child of God. The blessings are yours.

Prayer Points

1. In the name of Jesus, I unleash the fire of God against everything after my prosperity (Hebrews 12:29).
2. In the name of Jesus, I take my stand as a child of God and execute judgment on anything after my blessings (Psalm 149:6-9).
3. Father, in the name of Jesus, surround me now with Your impregnable wall as You have promised (Psalms 125:2).

Drinking Milk

If you see yourself drinking milk in your dream, what does it mean?

Interpretation

Since milk nourishes the body, this dream usually indicates good health. The Lord is restoring your health. You may have this dream especially if you are sick or bedridden. Prayers can help restore you to good health.

What To Do

- Give thanks to God.

- Read scriptures on healing: Matthew 8:17, Isaiah 53:5, Exodus 15:26.
- Pray for the manifestation of this dream.

Prayer Points

1. Thank You, Father, for healing me.
2. In the name of Jesus, I command a physical manifestation of this dream now (Ezekiel 12:23).
3. In the name of Jesus, God has sent His word. I am in good health now (Psalm 107:20).
4. In the name of Jesus, let every part of my body, soul, spirit, and bones be restored to good health now.
5. In the name of Jesus, I receive wholeness in every part of my body now (John 5:11).

CHAPTER 11

Fights, Contentions & Mishaps in Dreams

In this chapter, we will look at dreams where you experience fights or mishaps, and what to do about them. Have you ever had a dream where you were in a fight? If someone comes after you in a dream to fight you, it means you have something valuable. You are valuable. It doesn't matter what your situation is, you are very valuable. What you have or who you are is valuable to the person fighting you in the dream. That's why they want to eliminate you. Sometimes these fights in dreams feel so real that some people wake up very tired. Other times, an injury from the dream shows up in real life. Problems in dreams can have real-life effects.

Fights You Won

If you fought in a dream and won, what does it mean?

Interpretation

Dreams involving fights are usually about your life and health, but they could also be about other things. If you were injured in a fight in your dream, but you won, it's still okay. It means God has given you victory over a strong enemy. But there's more to do to make sure you don't win the battle but lose the war. If injuries are not treated, they could be as deadly as losing. Nevertheless, you will not lose any war in your life in Jesus' name.

What To Do

- Thank God for giving you victory.
- Strengthen your victory with strong prayers.
- Pray for complete healing and recovery.
- Pray the following prayers for at least three consecutive nights.

Prayer Points

1. Father, in the name of Jesus, thank You for giving me victory.
2. It is written: *"They will fight against you but will not overcome you, for I am with you and will rescue you," declares the LORD Jeremiah 1:19. (NIV)* Therefore, in the name of Jesus, I enforce my victory against fierce enemies fighting me in my dream. I overcome you now.
3. It is written: *"With God we will gain the victory, and he will trample down our enemies" Psalm 60:12.* Therefore, in the name of Jesus, I gain permanent victory over this enemy in my dream. You are trampled down underfoot now.
4. In the name of Jesus, it is written that nothing by any means would hurt me (Luke 10:19). Therefore, I declare quick healing and total recovery in my life now.

Fights You Lost

If you fought in a dream but lost, what does it mean?

Interpretation

This is not a good dream. It means the enemy has taken control of an important part of your life. You may start seeing things go very wrong if this dream is not dealt with, especially in your health. Even though this is not a good dream, don't be afraid.

What To Do

- When you wake up, don't be afraid at all. Be brave. If you could see Jesus in your room, He would tell you, "Fear not!"
- Spend time in praise and worship. This is the best way to show your faith. It helps you focus on God and strengthens your spirit. It ensures you don't pray out of fear.
- Pray strongly for at least 30 minutes, preferably an hour. Do this for three consecutive nights.

Prayer Points

1. Father, I magnify You because there is no one like You. You are stronger than the strongest. You have never lost any battle. You are the Man of War (Exodus 15:3).
2. It is written: *"Only by your power can we push back our enemies; only in your name can we trample our foes" Psalm 44:5.* Therefore, in the name of Jesus, I push back permanently in victory against every dream attack and trample them in the name of the Lord.
3. In the name of Jesus, I put on the whole armor of God. It is written: *"They will fight against you but will not overcome you, for I am with you and will rescue you," declares the LORD Jeremiah*

1:19. (NIV) Therefore, in the name of Jesus, I refuse to be defeated. Father, rescue me now.

4. It is written: *"But the Lord is with me as a mighty, awesome One. Therefore, my persecutors will stumble and will not prevail. They will be greatly ashamed, for they will not prosper. Their everlasting confusion will never be forgotten" Jeremiah 20:11 (NKJV).* Therefore, I command all my persecutors to stumble, be greatly ashamed, not prosper, and not prevail in Jesus' name.

5. It is written: *"No curse can touch Jacob; no magic has any power against Israel. For now, it will be said of Jacob, 'What wonders God has done for Israel!'" Numbers 23:23.* Therefore, I speak to every evil done against my health in my dream, be reversed now in Jesus' name.

6. Arise, O Lord, and let every enemy of my soul be scattered (Psalm 68:1).

Fights With No Conclusive Winner

Have you ever had a dream where you fought but there was no clear winner? You fought for a while, moving around, but couldn't win. What does it mean?

Interpretation

If you had a dream with no clear winner, it's not a good sign. You should always aim to win. Not winning means you're not stronger than the enemy, giving them a chance to regroup and fight you again.

What To Do

- Don't be afraid.
- Strengthen your faith in the Lord.

- Read and study scriptures that affirm your authority as a believer and pray with them. For example, 1 John 5:4, 1 John 4:4, Luke 10:19, Matthew 28:20, Ephesians 2:6, Romans 8:31.
- Pray for God's anointing to make you a warrior (Psalm 144:1).

Prayer Points

1. Father, thank You because greater is He that is in me than he that is in the world (1 John 4:4).
2. Father, in the name of Jesus, give me a warrior's anointing (Psalm 144:1).
3. By the authority given to me by Jesus, I now exercise complete control over every power fighting against me. Bow down now! (Luke 10:19).
4. As it is written, I trample on every power of the enemy fighting me in Jesus' name (Luke 10:19).
5. I go into the camp of every enemy fighting against me and inflict irreversible damage on them in Jesus' name.

Locked Gates or Shut Doors

If you dream of being behind a locked gate or a door shutting against you, what does it mean?

Interpretation

Doors or gates provide access. A gate or door shutting against you means that what is behind it belongs to you and is meant to enhance your life. However, the enemy intentionally shut the access because of you. In the book of Joshua 6:1, the Bible says: *"Now Jericho was securely shut up because of the children of Israel; none went out, and none came in." (NKJV)* Jericho was given to the children of Israel by God, but the enemy shut it against them.

What To Do

- ▸ Reflect. Are there opportunities that are hard for you to reach?
- ▸ Notice. Are you repeatedly failing exams or evaluations meant to advance you?
- ▸ Recall. Do you work hard on projects only for them to fall apart at the end?
- ▸ If any of these are true, you need to pray strongly.

Prayer Points

1. In the name of Jesus, every gate and door shut against me, be opened now (Psalms 24:7).
2. In the name of Jesus, every gate and door of iron shut against me, be broken to pieces (Psalms 107:16).
3. Father, in the name of Jesus, open doors and gates for me that can never be shut (Revelation 3:8).

Checkpoint, Strongman, Gatekeeper

Have you ever seen the police set up a checkpoint on a road, causing delays? This also happens spiritually in dreams. Have you experienced this in a dream or its variations? It doesn't matter if it happens on foot, in a car, train, bicycle, or any other way. The main idea is the same.

Interpretation

This dream means there is an enemy assigned to stop you from progressing and achieving your goals. You could have this dream after God has opened doors for you or answered your prayers. The person blocking you is like the Strongman Jesus mentioned in Luke 11:21-23. When the checkpoint is removed, you can freely access what's yours. Daniel experienced this with his prayer: *"Then he said, 'Don't be afraid, Daniel. Since the first day you began to pray for understanding and to humble yourself before your God, your request has been heard in heaven. I have come in answer to your prayer. But for twenty-one days the spirit prince of the kingdom of Persia blocked my way....' Daniel 10:12-13."* The Apostle Paul also experienced this: *"For a great and effective door has opened to me, and there are many adversaries." 1 Corinthians 16:9. (NKJV)*

What To Do

- Observe. Has your progress in life stalled?
- Note. Do you dream good dreams that don't come true?
- Pray aggressively for angelic help to remove every Strongman blocking your progress.

Prayer Points

1. Father, in the name of Jesus, command Your angels to remove anything hindering my prayers (Psalm 91:11).
2. Father, in the name of Jesus, send angels to fight against every adversary blocking my opportunities (Hebrews 1:14).
3. In the name of Jesus, I bind every strongman at work in my life (Matthew 18:18).
4. In the name of Jesus, I take hold of my possessions and all that belongs to me now.

Someone Pressing You While Sleeping

Sometimes people feel like someone is pressing down on them while they are sleeping. This can happen when they are very tired or at other times.

Interpretation

This dream means that witchcraft is oppressing you. If not addressed, it could lead to real physical injuries. It means when you are asleep, you are spiritually weak.

What To Do

- When you wake up, be strong and don't be afraid. Start praying.
- Build your spiritual strength. Begin a daily routine of reading the Bible and praying.
- Set alarms to remind you to pray at least three times daily.
- Pray for at least fifteen minutes before bedtime to strengthen your spirit.
- Avoid watching or listening to anything that could affect your spirit before bedtime.

Prayer Points

1. In the name of Jesus, I come against every witchcraft attack in my life. Be consumed by the fire of God (Hebrews 12:29).
2. In the name of Jesus, I cleanse my spirit, soul, and body with the blood of Jesus (1 John 1:7).
3. In the name of Jesus, I fortify my spirit. Be strengthened with the fire of the Holy Spirit (Ephesians 3:16).
4. In the name of Jesus, I command my spirit not to be weak while I sleep. Be a lion (Zechariah 12:8).
5. In the name of Jesus, Father, watch over me while I sleep because You never sleep (Psalm 121:4).

Nightmare

Do you have nightmares? A child of God should not be having nightmares. The Bible says, *"In peace I will lie down and sleep, for you alone, O LORD, will keep me safe." Psalm 4:8.* If you have nightmares, it's a sign of oppression. It shows that the devil has an opening into your spirit. Negative things can enter our lives through what we see, hear, say, eat, smell, or touch. Opening any of these gates allows the enemy access to your life. Sin can also give the enemy the right to oppress you.

What To Do

- Don't panic. There is still hope.
- Assess yourself. Have you opened any of these gates to the enemy? Close them.
- Identify any sin that gives Satan the right to oppress you. Repent and forsake it.
- Pray aggressively until the nightmares stop.

Prayer Points

1. Father, in the name of Jesus, thank You because with You my victory is guaranteed.
2. Father, in the name of Jesus, I close any gates that have been compromised in my life.
3. Father, in the name of Jesus, I confess and repent of the sin of _____ (name the sin). Forgive me.
4. In the name of Jesus, I invoke the blood of Jesus against every Satanic oppression in my life.
5. In the name of Jesus, I command every root of nightmare to quiet down now.
6. Holy Spirit of God, fill me completely, even while I am asleep.

Flying or Soaring

What does it mean if you see yourself flying or soaring in a dream?

Interpretation

"But those who wait on the Lord shall renew their strength; They shall mount up with wings like eagles, They shall run and not be weary, They shall walk and not faint." Isaiah 40:31. (NKJV)

As a child of God, if you dream of flying or soaring above obstacles, it is generally a good dream. It could mean that you have been empowered by the Holy Spirit to rise above challenges. It also means divine elevation and promotion. This is a sign that you have what it takes to overcome current challenges. However, if you find yourself flying aimlessly and in fear, it signifies witchcraft manipulation. This could lead to confusion and oppression by the enemy. If flying to a meeting, it indicates the spirit of witchcraft. Deliverance is needed.

What To Do

- Assess your life. If your dream indicates empowerment, give thanks to God.
- If it indicates manipulation, it means your prayer life is weak. Increase your prayer life.
- If it indicates the spirit of witchcraft, perform a self-deliverance with the prayers below or seek help from a minister of God equipped for deliverance.
- Pray aggressively with fasting for three nights if your dream indicates manipulation instead of empowerment.

Prayer Points

1. Father, in the name of Jesus, thank You for empowering me.
2. Father, in the name of Jesus, let me walk in and manifest the empowerment You have given me.
3. In the name of Jesus, I begin to soar over obstacles and challenges.
4. In the name of Jesus, I break every witchcraft spell over my life (Galatians 3:1).
5. In the name of Jesus, I invoke the blood of Jesus against every witchcraft manipulation.

DREAMS

6. With my hands on my head, I renounce every covenant with witchcraft in Jesus' name.
7. With my mouth open, I command every unclean spirit in my body to leave in the name of Jesus.
8. I confess that Jesus is the Lord and owner of my life. Therefore, every spirit of witchcraft defiling my spirit and body must leave in Jesus' name.

Falling

What does it mean if you dream about falling?

Interpretation

"for though the righteous fall seven times, they rise again..." Proverbs 24:16 (NIV).

In real life, falling is not good. It means you are losing your balance or stability. If you fall in a dream, it could mean demotion or losing importance. It could also mean you lack a helper as described in Ecclesiastes 4:10. Another interpretation is that your carelessness or lack of discretion could lead you into sin (1 Corinthians 10:12). Falling could also mean sickness if you don't pay attention to your health. If it is a heavy fall, it means a serious injury or death. But don't be afraid. There is a way out.

What to Do

- Start with your health. Is there anything of concern? Have you had a physical checkup lately?
- Besides your spouse, are you emotionally attached to anyone? Disconnect immediately.
- If single, do you have boundaries with the opposite sex?

- Do you lack a trusted companion? Begin to prayerfully search for one.
- Have you fallen? Now begin the journey of getting back up.

Prayer Points

1. Father, in the name of Jesus, restore me where I have fallen (Proverbs 24:16).
2. Father, in the name of Jesus, as I visit the doctors, let any hidden condition be exposed.
3. Father, in the name of Jesus, help me to be watchful and avoid every appearance of sin (1 Corinthians 10:12).
4. Father, in the name of Jesus, send me my trusted companion (Ecclesiastes 4:10).
5. In the name of Jesus, I will not fall from grace to grass (Genesis 39:12).

Losing Your Teeth

If you dream about losing your teeth and nothing is wrong with your teeth in real life, what does it mean?

Interpretation

"Instead of your shame you shall have double honor..." Isaiah 61:7. (NKJV)

If you dream about losing your teeth, it has significant implications. Our teeth are part of the facial structures that make us attractive and approachable. A good set of teeth gives us confidence and helps us speak, eat, and drink properly. Losing a good set of teeth in a dream could mean an attack on your confidence and communication skills. You may start becoming terrified or fearful, and people may misunderstand whatever you say. If you are single, losing your teeth in a dream indicates a satanic attack on your relationships, potentially preventing them from lasting or leading to marriage. If you are married, your spouse may no longer find you desirable.

What to Do

- Are you single or married? What is currently happening with relationships in your life?
- Do you feel terrified lately?
- Pray the prayers below with fasting for three nights. Then continue praying at least three times every day until it is resolved, especially if the dream keeps recurring.

Prayer Points

1. Thank You, Father, because victory is mine.
2. In the name of Jesus, I come against whatever has been done to cause me shame.
3. In the name of Jesus, every attack on my confidence and communication fails now.
4. In the name of Jesus, every attack on my relationships fails now.
5. In the name of Jesus, every attack on my marriage fails now.
6. Father, in the name of Jesus, according to Your word, instead of shame, give me double honor and restore me now (Isaiah 61:7).

CHAPTER 12

Exes, Past Life & Death Dreams

In this chapter we will explore dreams about exes, past life and death dreams. If you see any of these dreams, what could they mean for you?

Seeing An Ex In A Dream

Some people dream about their ex-partners, whether an ex-wife, ex-husband, ex-boyfriend, or ex-girlfriend. Even if you're currently married or have moved on to someone else, dreaming about an ex can happen. What does this mean?

Interpretation

- **Once:** If you dream of your ex once after moving on, and the dream isn't sexual or harmful, it's likely not an issue. It's probably because you've been used to having them in your life. However, if the dream is sexual, it could be a demonic presence disguising as your ex to oppress you. Such dreams tend to recur and signify spiritual attack. If not demonic, it may mean you still have lingering feelings or sexual attraction toward your ex.

- **Frequent Appearance:** If you frequently dream about your ex (non-sexual), consider how the relationship ended. Was it on friendly terms, or was there hostility or animosity? Hostility or unresolved issues can manifest in your dreams. However, if there's no hostility and the dreams persist, it might indicate soul ties, especially if you were sexually intimate with your exes.

What To Do

- Reflect on which scenario applies to your life.
- If you still feel attracted to your ex while married, address this prayerfully and wisely to prevent issues.
- If you have sexual dreams involving your ex, consider self-deliverance to break soul ties or seek help from a trusted spiritual leader.
- If there is hostility between you and your ex, forgive and seek God's peace.
- Pray continuously using the prayer points below until the dreams stop.

Prayer Points

1. Father, in the name of Jesus, thank You for Your unfailing love that I can always rely on (Lamentations 3:22-23).
2. Father, in the name of Jesus, I confess my sins of _____ (insert sin). Please forgive me (1 John 1:9).
3. Father, Your Word says You won't reject a broken heart (Psalm 51:17). Please be merciful to me and help me now.

4. Father, in the name of Jesus, I forgive all those who have offended me, including my ex, and I release them.
5. As I place my hand on my head, let the power that raised Jesus from the dead flow through me now and deliver me from every satanic oppression in my dreams (Romans 8:11).
6. By the blood of Jesus, I break every covenant, oath, agreement, and contract connecting me to any ex, in Jesus' name.
7. By the blood of Jesus, I renounce and break every soul tie connecting me to exes in the name of Jesus.
8. In the name of Jesus, I break the power of lust, and the hold sin has over me now.
9. In the name of Jesus, anything in me that attracts oppression in my dreams, be exposed by the fire of God.

Old House/Former House, Elementary School, High School

Many people dream about being in their old house, elementary school, high school, or even their former workplace. What do these dreams mean?

Interpretation

Dreaming of being back in your old house or school indicates the spirit of backwardness and stagnation in your life. It suggests that although you may appear to have progressed physically, spiritually, you are still stuck where you started. This stagnation could be generational or specific to you. However, God's plan is for your life to improve and not regress. Jesus said, *"The thief's purpose is to steal and kill and destroy. My purpose is to give them a rich and satisfying life" John 10:10.*

What To Do

- Reflect on your life. Do you feel stuck in the same spot?

- Do you find yourself taking one step forward and then three steps back?
- Break the spiritual connection between you and your past.
- Because this can be a persistent issue, I recommend praying aggressively nightly for at least three nights. You can find inspiration in the story of Jacob in Genesis 32:22-31.

Prayer Points

1. Jesus, thank You for promising me a rich and satisfying life (John 10:10).
2. Father, in the name of Jesus, end the work of the spirit of stagnation and backwardness in my life and family.
3. In the name of Jesus, I break every spiritual connection between my current self and my old self.
4. Father, in the name of Jesus, remove my reproach just as You did for the children of Israel (Joshua 5:9).
5. In the name of Jesus, I move forward (Exodus 14:15).

Dreaming About Dead Loved Ones

When we lose someone we love, we often feel broken and yearn to be reunited with them. The devil exploits this vulnerability. Dreaming about a deceased loved one is common. However, if it happens frequently, it could indicate a problem.

Interpretation

The devil may send a familiar spirit that looks like your loved one in your dream. He knows your guard will be down around them. This impostor might give you instructions, feed you, etc. It's not your loved one, but an evil spirit using their image to deceive and gain access to your life. Unless you have the gift of discerning spirits, you might fall into this trap.

DREAMS

Familiar spirits can provide accurate information about you and your deceased loved one. For example, in the Bible, King Saul consulted a witch who summoned the dead prophet Samuel (1 Samuel 28:3-25). If not addressed, such dreams can lead to death, insanity, depression, terminal diseases, or demonic oppression.

What To Do

- Ask the Lord to heal your broken heart to prevent the enemy from exploiting it.
- Rebuke the spirit of death over your life.
- Drive away familiar spirits from your dreams.
- If you have taken something that belonged to a deceased person, return it immediately.

Prayer Points

1. Father, in the name of Jesus, heal my broken heart and make my spirit strong.
2. In the name of Jesus, I rebuke the spirit of death over my life (Romans 8:2).
3. In the name of Jesus, I drive away familiar spirits from my dreams.
4. Father, in the name of Jesus, expose anything that attracts familiar spirits into my life.

Casket, Coffin, Grave, Cemetery

Dreaming of a casket, coffin, grave, or cemetery is not a good sign.

Interpretation

These dreams signify the spirit of death. However, you can cancel it through prayer.

What To Do

- ▸ Do not panic upon waking up.
- ▸ Start praying immediately.
- ▸ Pray for at least three consecutive nights.
- ▸ If the dream repeats, add fasting to your prayers.

Prayer Points

1. In the name of Jesus, I rebuke the spirit of death. Leave my life.
2. In the name of Jesus, I cancel every appointment with the grave.
3. By the blood of Jesus, I cancel every appointment with death.
4. In the name of Jesus, I shall not die but live and declare the works of the Lord (Psalm 118:17, NKJV).
5. In the name of Jesus, God will satisfy me with long life and show me His salvation (Psalm 91:16).

CHAPTER 13

Elevator, Watch & Phone Dreams

In this chapter, we will explore some other common dreams that you should not ignore. Sometimes, some people often see elevators, watches or phones in their dreams and don't know what they mean. As ordinary as they may seem, these things contain valuable information for the dreamer.

Stopped Elevator

If you dream of being in a stopped elevator, what does it mean?

Interpretation

If you're in an elevator that has stopped moving, it signifies stagnation. Your progress has halted, and all your hard work would lead to nothing.

What To Do

- ▸ Pray against stagnation.
- ▸ Pray against spiritual limitations.

Prayer Points

1. In the name of Jesus, I break every stronghold of stagnation in my life with Your mighty hand (1 Peter 5:6).
2. In the name of Jesus, I break every hold of witchcraft bewitchment over my life (Isaiah 10:27).
3. In the name of Jesus, I move forward by the Spirit of the Lord (1 Kings 18:46).
4. Father, in the name of Jesus, give me speed (1 Kings 18:46).

Elevator Going Down

If you dream of being in an elevator going down? What does this mean?

Interpretation

Dreaming of an elevator going down signifies demotion. It indicates a fall from grace if not actively dealt with. Your journey in life should be upward (Proverbs 4:18).

What To Do

- ▸ Observe if you're slacking in your work.
- ▸ Note if you've developed any harmful habits affecting your performance.
- ▸ Pray aggressively to stop this downward trend.

Prayer Points

1. In the name of Jesus, I arrest and send the spirit of demotion out of my life (Mark 16:17).

2. In the name of Jesus, any generational limitation over my life is broken now (Deuteronomy 33:6).
3. In the name of Jesus, I cancel every spiritual manipulation intended to bring me down (Joshua 14:11).
4. In the name of Jesus, I render every demotion ineffective (Isaiah 54:17).

Elevator Going Up

If you are in an elevator that is going up, what does this mean?

Interpretation

If you're in an elevator going up, this is a positive sign. It indicates promotion, elevation, and a change of status, which is God's desire for all His children (2 Corinthians 3:18).

What To Do

- Be expectant and rejoice.
- Cancel any hindrances that may come.
- Pray aggressively for the manifestation.

Prayer Points

1. Father, thank You for Your good plans for me (Jeremiah 29:11).
2. In the name of Jesus, I cancel any interference from the prince of the power of the air that may want to block this dream from manifesting (Ephesians 2:2).
3. In the name of Jesus, I cancel every spiritual manipulation intended to bring me down (Joshua 14:11).
4. In the name of Jesus, I command this dream to manifest without delay (Ezekiel 12:23).

Climbing A Ladder or Stairs

If you were climbing a ladder, or a flight of stairs in your dream, what does it mean?

Interpretation

"The steps of a good man are ordered by the Lord, And He delights in his way." Psalms 37:23.

Dreaming of climbing a ladder or stairs usually indicates promotion, elevation, and progress. If you climb with ease, you will reach the next level without struggling. If you struggle, your progress might be difficult due to ignorance or the enemy's attack.

What To Do

- Thank God for the dream.
- Pray for its manifestation.
- Identify if your struggles are due to ignorance or attacks from the enemy.
- Seek the correct information if you struggle.
- Break any yokes or burdens on you.

Prayer Points

1. Father, thank You for this dream.
2. Jesus, according to Your word, remove every burden the enemy has put on me (Matthew 11:28).
3. In the name of Jesus, I command every yoke of struggle and difficulty to be broken now (Isaiah 10:27).
4. In the name of Jesus, I begin to enjoy smooth and effortless progress, promotion, and elevation in life.
5. Father, in the name of Jesus, by Your Holy Spirit, open my spiritual understanding (Ephesians 1:18).

Wearing A Watch/Given A Watch

Have you dreamed of wearing a watch or that someone gave you a watch, what does it mean?

Interpretation

Dreaming of wearing a watch or receiving one indicates the need to be time conscious.

What To Do

- Start doing things on time and stop procrastinating.
- Remember that the time to accomplish your goals is limited.

Prayer Points

1. Father, in the name of Jesus, help me to do things on time.
2. Father, in the name of Jesus, help me to do redeem my time.

Stopped Clock or Watch

If you look at a clock or watch in your dream and it stops working, what does it mean?

Interpretation

If you dream of a clock or watch that stopped working, it signifies stagnation and lack of progress. If you're working on a project or business, it means the enemy has obstructed your progress, and your efforts will be in vain.

What To Do

- Address your situation with prayers

Prayer Points

1. In the name of Jesus, I destroy every obstruction on my path to success.

2. In the name of Jesus, I drive out every spirit of stagnation in my life.
3. In the name of Jesus, I command my spiritual clock to start working properly again.

Clock or Watch Approaching 12

If you look at a clock or watch in your dream and see that, it is approaching twelve, what does it mean?

Interpretation

If you dream of a clock or watch approaching twelve, it indicates the window of opportunity is closing. You have less time to complete something important. It could also be a sign of premature death.

What To Do

- Start taking steps towards your goal.
- Pray against premature death.

Prayer Points

1. In the name of Jesus, I resist every spirit of procrastination.
2. In the name of Jesus, I cancel every plan for premature death in my life.

Clock or Watch Working Properly

If you are in a dream and your attention is drawn to a clock or watch in your dream that is working properly, what does it mean?

Interpretation

If you dream of a clock or watch working properly, it means everything is working according to God's plan. Despite challenges, you are progressing and still on the right track.

What To Do

- ▸ Thank God for the message.
- ▸ Do things on time.
- ▸ Pray that your life's journey continues according to God's timing.
- ▸ Ask for the grace to trust, believe, and wait on God despite what you see.
- ▸ Avoid any shortcuts or quick schemes.

Prayer Points

1. Father, thank You for this message.
2. Father, in the name of Jesus, let my life's journey continue uninterrupted in Your plans.
3. Father, in the name of Jesus, I ask for the grace to trust, believe, and wait on You despite what I see.
4. Father, in the name of Jesus, help me avoid the temptation of shortcuts or quick schemes outside Your plans.

Phone

Have you seen a phone in your dream? Wondering what it means? Let's clear up the confusion.

Interpretation

In the physical world, a phone holds contact information and delivers news and information from various sources. If you were given a new phone in your dream, it could mean you will gain access to new information or contacts. How did you feel after receiving the phone?

- ▸ Bad: It indicates bad news.
- ▸ Good: It indicates good news.
- ▸ Neutral: It's just informational.

What To Do

- ▸ If you felt bad, pray to God to cancel the bad news or give you the grace to bear it if it's His will.
- ▸ If you felt good, pray for the manifestation of the good news.
- ▸ If neutral, pray for the grace to exercise discretion.
- ▸ Stay open to new contacts and information that could lead to something better.

Prayer Points

1. Father, in the name of Jesus, cancel any news that is not in Your will for my life.
2. In the name of Jesus, I command good news and good contacts to come to me now (Proverbs 25:25).
3. In the name of Jesus, I will not miss my day of manifestation of good things (Luke 1:11,13).
4. Father, hasten the performance of this dream in my life now (Jeremiah 1:12).
5. Father, grant me wisdom in my affairs (Ecclesiastes 10:10).

Lost Phone

What if you dreamed that you lost your phone? This isn't a good sign, but it can be fixed.

Interpretation

Losing a phone in the physical world means losing contacts and important information. If you lose your phone in a dream, it signifies the potential loss of valuable information and contacts in your life if not addressed.

What To Do

- Ensure you are dealing with those around you with integrity and honesty.
- Avoid greed and actions that could lead to betrayal or broken trust.
- If you are a leader, ensure those working with you are honest and not cutting corners.
- Pray aggressively against satanic manipulation and witchcraft.

Prayer Points

1. Father, in the name of Jesus, help me overcome every temptation of greed and betrayal.
2. Father, in the name of Jesus, let those working for me be filled with the Spirit of the fear of the Lord (Isaiah 11:2).
3. In the name of Jesus, I cancel every form of witchcraft in my life (Galatians 3:1).
4. In the name of Jesus, I recover every good thing stolen from me (Joel 2:25).
5. In the name of Jesus, I will not lose any valuable information and contacts.

CHAPTER 14

Transportation Dreams (Cars, Plane, Train)

In this chapter, we'll explore dreams about transportation, like cars, trains, airplanes, and ships. These dreams often reflect your life, health, or progress, so they should be taken seriously. Their state or condition also has meanings.

- A car might symbolize your life, especially your health.
- It could represent your progress or journey through life.
- It might also indicate a leadership position if you're driving with others in the car.

Car/Automobile with Tires Off

If you dream about your car losing one or all its tires, take it seriously.

Interpretation

This dream usually relates to your health.

- If the tires come off one by one, it means your health is declining.
- If all the tires come off at once, it implies serious illness or even death if not addressed.
- If the car starts with the tires off, it indicates stagnation in life.

What to Do

- Visit a doctor for a health checkup.
- Pray against sickness and disease in your body.
- Pray against stagnation in life.

Prayer Points

1. In the name of Jesus, I command every spirit of sickness and disease in my body to leave (Mark 16:18).
2. In the name of Jesus, I command every debilitating disease to stop (Psalms 107:20).
3. In the name of Jesus, I declare my health restored (Proverbs 4:22).
4. Father, in the name of Jesus, deliver me from evil (Matthew 6:13).
5. In the name of Jesus, I remove anything causing stagnation in my life.

Driving Over Water

If you dream about driving your car on a bridge over a large body of water, it has a meaning for you.

Interpretation

God is telling you that your life's journey or current situation might be frightening, but don't be afraid. He has given you the victory to rise above it. If the water is calm, it means your journey will be smooth.

What to Do

- Read scriptures about courage to be strengthened.
- Pray for courage and strength.
- Pray for a smooth journey.

Prayer Points

1. Father, in the name of Jesus, strengthen my spirit, soul, and body (Ephesians 3:16).
2. Father, in the name of Jesus, send Your angels ahead of me in my life's journey (Psalms 91:11-12).
3. Father, in the name of Jesus, give me victory always (1 Corinthians 15:57).
4. Father, in the name of Jesus, smooth my journey and give me rest (Exodus 33:14).

Car In Traffic

Dreaming about being stuck in traffic while driving a car is not just an ordinary dream.

Interpretation

If you dream that your car is stuck in traffic, it implies delay in your life. It means the enemy is resisting your progress. You may experience delays in reaching important milestones and struggle in your career, business, ministry, or marriage.

Transportation Dreams (Cars, Plane, Train)

What to Do

- Assess your life to see if you are making timely progress.
- Pray against the spirit of delay and hard labor.
- Command your path to be cleared.
- Pray for angelic assistance.

Prayer Points

1. In the name of Jesus, I command every yoke of delay and slow progress in my life to be broken (Isaiah 10:27).
2. In the name of Jesus, I command every yoke of hard labor and struggle to be broken (Matthew 11:28-29).
3. In the name of Jesus, I rebuke the spirit of delay and hard labor (Luke 10:19).
4. In the name of Jesus, angels of God, clear my path in life (Hebrews 1:14).

Driver Changing

What if you are being driven by someone in your dream and then the driver changes? This meaning depends on your current situation, whether the person is known or not. The context, whether a work environment or marriage also matters.

Interpretation

If you dream about being driven by someone else and then the driver changes, the meaning depends on your situation.

- **Single:** If you are a single woman, this dream means the guy you are with is not right for you. If you are a single man, it means the woman you are with is not right for you.

- **Married:** If you are a married woman, this dream symbolizes the potential loss of your husband through death, separation, or divorce. If you are a married man, it indicates the potential loss of your wife through death, separation, or divorce.

What to Do

- If single, reassess your relationship and ask God for direction.
- If married, pray against the loss of your marriage or spouse.

Prayer Points

1. Father, in the name of Jesus, lead me to do Your will.
2. In the name of Jesus, I come against losses in my marriage.
3. In the name of Jesus, I cover my marriage and my spouse with the name of the Lord.
4. In the name of Jesus, I cancel the spirit of death in my marriage.

Driver Changed To You

What if the driver of a bus or a car that you are in with other passengers was changed to you? What does this mean?

Interpretation

This means that you are being promoted to be a leader. Note the context whether it happened. Is it with family members or colleagues? The environment where it happened is where you will be leading.

What To Do

- Pray against losses in your family.
- Pray for the spirit of wisdom to lead.

Prayer Points

1. Father, in the name of Jesus, let there be no loss in my family (Psalms 91:10-11).
2. Father, in the name of Jesus, fill me with wisdom, knowledge, and understanding to be a good leader (James 1:5).

Driving At Night Without Lights

If you dream about driving at night but your lights are out, what does this mean?

Interpretation

In real life, driving at night without lights is dangerous because you have no guidance. Spiritually, it means you lack God's guidance. The Bible says, *"Your word is a lamp to my feet, And a light to my path." Psalm 119:105. (NKJV)* So, this dream means you're running your life on your own terms, which could lead to problems.

What to Do

- Think about decisions you've made without consulting God.
- Reflect on any instructions from God that you've ignored.
- Commit to being close to God. Start with daily Bible reading and prayer.
- Decide to obey God no matter what.
- Pray for spiritual understanding.

Prayer Points

1. Father, forgive me for making decisions without involving You or disobeying You (1 John 1:9).
2. Father, in the name of Jesus, give me a new heart that delights in obeying You always (Ezekiel 36:26).

3. In the name of Jesus, I receive a desire to crave God's word (1 Peter 2:2).
4. In the name of Jesus, let the spirit of prayer and supplication come upon me (Zechariah 12:10).
5. Father, in the name of Jesus, open my spiritual understanding by Your Holy Spirit (Ephesians 1:18).

Train, Bus, Airplane

Seeing a train, bus, or airplane in your dream, what do they mean?

Interpretation

A train, bus, or airplane in a dream usually represents your journey in life.

Crowded Train, Bus, or Airplane

If you see yourself trying to get on a crowded train, bus, or airplane, what does it mean?

Interpretation

This signifies struggle in life. It means whatever task or project you're working on will be hard to accomplish. Reaching the next level in your life will be challenging. It could also mean an attack from the enemy to delay you. However, it doesn't mean you should give up.

What to Do

- Don't panic. Thank God for showing this to you.
- Pray and ask if you should continue your current path.
- If you're convinced it's from God, ask for strength to continue.
- Pray against any attack from the enemy.

Prayer Points

1. Thank You, Father, for revealing my life to me.
2. Father, in the name of Jesus, show me if You want me to continue this path.
3. Father, in the name of Jesus, I receive strength to continue the path You have for me.
4. In the name of Jesus, Satan, get your hands off my life and progress (James 4:7).
5. In Jesus' name, I cast down everything done to make my journey hard (2 Corinthians 10:5).

Missing A Train, Bus, Flight

If you miss your train, bus, or flight in your dream, what does it mean?

Interpretation

Missing your train, bus, or flight signifies missing opportunities in your life. It means missing important moments like promotions or marital blessings. This could be due to carelessness or manipulation by the enemy, with manipulation being more common.

What to Do

- Thank God for showing this to you.
- Reflect on areas where you might be careless.
- Pray against manipulation in your life.

Prayer Points:

1. Thank You, Father, for revealing my life to me.
2. Father, in the name of Jesus, show me any areas where I am careless.

3. In the name of Jesus, I take authority over any manipulation in my life. I cancel all their operations in Jesus' name.
4. In the name of Jesus, I recover every missed opportunity.

Delayed Train, Bus, Flight

If your train, bus, or flight is delayed in your dream, what does it mean?

Interpretation

A delayed train, bus, or flight in a dream means there's a restriction on your life in the spiritual realm. This can show up physically as delayed marriage, promotions, financial success, or childbearing. It's an attack from the enemy.

What to Do:

- Thank God for revealing this to you.
- Reflect on areas of your life where things aren't happening on time.
- Pray against the spirit of delay.

Prayer Points:

1. Thank You, Father, for showing my life to me.
2. In the name of Jesus, I command the spirit of delay in my _____ (mention the area) to lose its hold now (Matthew 18:18).
3. In the name of Jesus, I break every stronghold of delay in my _____ (mention the area) now.
4. In the name of Jesus, I command everything in my life to start working on time.

Transportation Dreams (Cars, Plane, Train)

On the Wrong Train, Bus, Flight

If you dream about being on the wrong train, bus, or flight, what does it mean?

Interpretation

Being on the wrong train, bus, or flight in a dream means there's a spirit of confusion and anti-progress forces affecting your life, rerouting your journey. It could also mean you're ignorant in certain areas of your life.

What to Do

- Thank God for revealing this to you.
- Reflect on areas of your life where you might be heading in the wrong direction.
- Pray against the spirit of confusion and anti-progress forces.

Prayer Points

1. Thank You, Father, for revealing this to me.
2. In the name of Jesus, I come against every spirit of confusion in my _____ (mention the area). Leave now (Psalm 18:45).
3. In the name of Jesus, I break every stronghold of anti-progress forces in my _____ (mention the area) now.
4. In the name of Jesus, I decree clarity in my life now.

CHAPTER 15

Clothing and Shoes Dreams

In this chapter, we will look at dreams about nakedness, clothing and shoes. Though they are common, their meanings vary.

Nakedness While Others Are Clothed

If you dream that you are fully naked while others around you are fully clothed, what does it mean?

Interpretation

This dream means shame, disgrace, humiliation, and poverty. If you were forcefully stripped naked, it could mean that you are about to be betrayed or that there are demonic forces stronger than you trying to shame you.

Clothing and Shoes Dreams

This dream can be triggered by generational and chronic poverty or debt. If it's a recurring dream, generational poverty might be at work in your life.

What To Do

- Don't be afraid; God reveals things through dreams.
- Look at your family history. Are there patterns of shame and humiliation?
- Examine yourself. Are you in heavy debt and struggling financially?
- Use discretion in your actions.
- Pray morning, afternoon, and evening if it's a chronic or generational issue until the dream stops.

Prayer Points

1. In the name of Jesus, I cancel every effort to bring me public shame, disgrace, and humiliation.
2. Father, in the name of Jesus, uproot every symbolic tree and seed of generational poverty in my life. *"Jesus replied, 'Every plant not planted by my heavenly Father will be uprooted.'"* Matthew 15:13.
3. Father, in the name of Jesus, deliver me from powers stronger than me. *"He rescued me from my powerful enemies, from those who hated me and were too strong for me."* Psalm 18:19.
4. It is written, *"Instead of shame and dishonor, you will enjoy a double share of honor. You will possess a double portion of prosperity in your land, and everlasting joy will be yours."* Isaiah 61:7. Therefore, in the name of Jesus, instead of shame and dishonor, I will enjoy a double share of honor.

Someone Naked Next To You

If you dream and see a fully naked man or woman next to you, what does it mean?

Interpretation

This is not a good dream. It is often caused by marine spirits, which are satanic forces operating in the seas or any large body of water. In Matthew 8:24-26, a storm arose from the powers in the sea that threatened to sink Jesus' boat, but He calmed the storm.

If you have this dream, it indicates that the spirit of lust and sexual immorality is at work in your life. Have you watched pornography, masturbated, slept with different people, read pornographic materials, or listened to explicit music? These actions open the door for those spirits to enter your life, leading to a polluted spiritual life and giving the devil legal authority to afflict you.

What To Do

- Don't panic.
- Check your life. Do you struggle with the spirit of lust? Be accountable to someone.
- If you struggle with fornication or adultery, seek counseling or deliverance.
- Pray fervently.

Prayer Points

1. Father, in the name of Jesus, forgive me for engaging in lust.
2. Father, in the name of Jesus, have mercy on me.
3. In the name of Jesus, I command the spirit of lust to leave my life now (Matthew 16:17).

4. In the name of Jesus, every yoke and chain of lust and sexual immorality over my life, be broken now (Matthew 11:28-30).
   5. Every power that the spirit of lust, pornography, fornication, or adultery has over me, be broken in Jesus' name (Romans 6:14).
   6. I command every activity of marine spirits in my life to stop now in Jesus' name.

Someone Having Sex With You

If you dream of someone being intimate with you, it's not a good sign. Consider the following: Was it consensual, meaning you didn't resist? Were you too tired to resist? Or were you forced against your will?

Interpretation

Consensual: If it was consensual or you were too tired to resist, it could mean the spirit of lust and immorality is at work. It could also mean you've been bewitched. If you've engaged in activities that invite these spirits, pray the same prayers as for seeing a fully naked person next to you.

Non-Consensual: If it wasn't consensual, it indicates the spirit of lust or marine spirits are oppressing you. If you're single, it could prevent you from getting married or lead to failed relationships. If you're married, it could cause dissatisfaction with your spouse or make you dislike intimacy.

Do you struggle with lust while awake but don't act on it? Do you find it hard to keep your eyes or thoughts pure? This spirit might be buried in your soul. While you control it when awake, you can't control it while asleep, attracting the spirit of lust.

Has someone with moral failings prayed for you? This could transfer the spirit to you. Another possibility is that you've been bewitched, or a spell was cast on you.

What To Do

- Take control of your life by reading the Bible daily. An audio Bible can help.
- Avoid reading, listening to, or watching anything that could arouse you. It can resurface in your sleep.
- Avoid preachers or ministers with moral failings from laying hands on you to prevent spirit transfer.
- Place your hands on your head and pray the following warfare prayers.

Prayer Points

1. Father, cleanse me from all filthiness by the blood of Your Son Jesus Christ.
2. My body is the temple of God. Therefore, spirit of lust, immorality, and every spirit defiling this temple, come under the wrath of God now in Jesus' name (1 Corinthians 3:16-17).
3. My spirit is one with the Lord and united with the Lord (1 Corinthians 6:17). Therefore, I seal off pathways of illegal access to my body now in Jesus' name.
4. I effect my deliverance in every area where I am a lawful captive of marine spirits in Jesus' name (Isaiah 49:24-26).
5. I confess that my body, soul, and spirit are the Lord's. Holy Spirit, exercise Your ownership over my life (1 Corinthians 3:17).

Half-Dressed

If you dream that you are half-dressed, either missing your top or bottom, what does it mean?

Interpretation

It could mean that while part of your life is okay, another part is shameful or a disgrace. In reality, your life might be just average. It could also mean you're not putting your best effort into what you do. Finally, it might indicate that demonic powers are trying to bring you down or keep you average.

What To Do

- Evaluate your life. Are you giving your best effort or just coasting?
- Seek knowledge where you are struggling and commit to applying it (John 8:32).
- Pray the following prayers.

Prayer Points

1. Holy Spirit, open my spiritual eyes to see where I lack knowledge.
2. In the name of Jesus, I will not be put to shame, disgrace, or dishonor (Romans 10:11).
3. In the name of Jesus, I neutralize every attempt to bring me down.
4. Father, in the name of Jesus, clothe me with Your glory wherever I am spiritually half-dressed (Genesis 3:21).

Clothes

Clothes have significant spiritual meanings. They can represent your social status and your standing before God. Clothes are often used in scriptures to convey messages.

New Clothes

If you dream about receiving or buying new clothes, what does it mean?

Interpretation

New clothes, whether given to you or bought, mean that your status and position will soon change. God is elevating you to a better position. Remember Joseph? When he was to appear before Pharaoh, his prison clothes were changed, and he never wore them again.

What To Do

- Rejoice and be expectant.
- Be diligent and continue to work hard on your talents, gifts, skills, and abilities. They will open doors of elevation for you.
- Pray for this good dream to become a reality.

Prayer Points

1. Father, thank You for remembering me (1 Samuel 2:21).
2. In the name of Jesus, let my talents, gifts, skills, and abilities make room for me before great and noble people (Proverbs 18:16).
3. In the name of Jesus, my talents, gifts, skills, and abilities will not remain hidden (Genesis 41:14).
4. Father, in the name of Jesus, watch over this dream and make it come true in my life (Jeremiah 1:12).
5. In the name of Jesus, I declare divine elevation, promotion, lifting, recognition, and a change of status for me now (Job 22:28).

Clothing and Shoes Dreams

Rags or Clothes With Holes

If you dream about wearing rags or clothes with holes, what does it mean?

Interpretation

This dream indicates poverty. It means spiritually you are wearing rags, and your life will be responding to poverty. If you are currently successful, it signals that demotion, disappointment, and poverty could be ahead if not addressed. Something has been set to make you poor. Like a thermostat regulates temperature, it will regulate your life and progress, bringing you down if not dealt with immediately.

What To Do

- Commit to praying aggressively.
- Pray at least three times daily until you feel relief in your spirit, or the dream stops.

Prayer Points

1. In the name of Jesus, I remove every rag that I may be wearing spiritually (Mark 10:50).
2. Father, in the name of Jesus, I set on fire everything put in place to bring me down (Hebrews 12:29).
3. Father, in the name of Jesus, change my spiritual clothes. Remove whatever repels prosperity and opportunities from me (Joshua 5:9).
4. Father, in the name of Jesus, clothe me with Your glory (John 17:22).

Stolen Shoes or Missing Shoes

Shoes complement our outfits and enable smooth mobility. Without shoes, walking is uncomfortable, tedious, and hard. Anything stolen in a dream is from the devil, meaning what was rightfully yours has been taken. The Bible says that Satan comes to do three things: steal, kill, and destroy

(John 10:10). So, what could stolen shoes symbolize in a dream? It symbolizes many things.

Interpretation

- **Foundational Problems:** Because shoes are close to the ground, it could mean foundational problems, especially chronic poverty. Foundational problems are negative patterns inherited from your parents or past generations, making progress in life difficult and fruitless.
- **Loss of a Spouse:** Stolen shoes could mean the loss of a spouse if the person is married. When someone wears shoes, they become one with the shoes and travel together. The Bible says that when a couple marries, they become one (Genesis 2:24). Losing a pair of shoes could mean the enemy is after your spouse.
- **Confusion in Life:** It could also indicate an attack by the devil to cause confusion in your life. Imagine needing to attend an important event but not finding the right shoes. It causes confusion and stops you in your tracks, halting your progress.

What To Do

- Examine your family history for negative patterns and write them down.
- If married, note anything unusual about your spouse and write it down.
- Identify any areas of confusion in your life, especially regarding the next step, and write it down.
- Pray fervently. Due to the severity, consider fasting and praying for three days, and praying nightly from 11 PM for at least an hour each night.

Prayer Points

1. Father, in the name of Jesus, I end every negative generational pattern in my family line that affects me or my children. I am a new creature in Christ (2 Corinthians 5:17).
2. In the name of Jesus, I terminate every inherited generational liability in my life and my children's lives.
3. In the name of Jesus, I command complete restoration of every good thing the enemy has stolen from my generation, me, and my family now (John 10:10).
4. In the name of Jesus, I cancel premature death and every attack of the devil on my marriage.
5. In the name of Jesus, I cancel every attack of the devil on my progress.

30-DAY DREAM INTERPRETATION JOURNAL

30-Day Dream Interpretation Journal

DATE:
Easy Recall Title:
Observation & Action:

People: **Animal:**   **Place:**

Event: **Number:**   **Color:**

Emotion/Feeling Fearful   Angry   Happy   Sad
(Circle One):   /Scared

Worried   Confused   Neutral   Peaceful   Other:

Focus: Me   Someone Else - Who?   Thing – What?

Relatable Context in Life:

Interpretation:

Recurring Good Dream? = Certainty Chances Increases
Recurring Bad Dream? = Not Properly Addressed

Conclusion   Warning   FYI   Future   Current   TBD
(Circle   (Prophetic)
One):   Past

Prayer Points

1.

2.

3.

150

DREAMS

DATE:
Easy Recall Title:
Observation & Action:

People: **Animal:**   **Place:**

Event: **Number:**   **Color:**

Emotion/Feeling   Fearful   Angry   Happy   Sad
(Circle One):   /Scared

Worried   Confused   Neutral   Peaceful   Other:

Focus: Me   Someone Else -   Thing – What?
                                Who?

Relatable Context in Life:

Interpretation:

Recurring Good Dream? = Certainty Chances Increases
Recurring Bad Dream? = Not Properly Addressed

Conclusion	Warning	FYI	Future	Current	TBD
(Circle			(Prophetic)		
One):			Past		

Prayer Points

1.

2.

3.

30-Day Dream Interpretation Journal

DATE:
Easy Recall Title:
Observation & Action:

People: **Animal:** **Place:**

Event: **Number:** **Color:**

Emotion/Feeling (Circle One): Fearful/Scared Angry Happy Sad

Worried Confused Neutral Peaceful Other:

Focus: Me Someone Else - Who? Thing – What?

Relatable Context in Life:

Interpretation:

Recurring Good Dream? = Certainty Chances Increases
Recurring Bad Dream? = Not Properly Addressed

Conclusion (Circle One): Warning FYI Future (Prophetic) Past Current TBD

Prayer Points

1.

2.

3.

DREAMS

DATE:
Easy Recall Title:
Observation & Action:

People: **Animal:**   **Place:**

Event: **Number:**   **Color:**

Emotion/Feeling   Fearful   Angry   Happy   Sad
(Circle One):   /Scared

Worried   Confused   Neutral   Peaceful   Other:

Focus: Me   Someone Else -   Thing – What?
                                Who?

Relatable Context in Life:

Interpretation:

Recurring Good Dream? = Certainty Chances Increases

Recurring Bad Dream? = Not Properly Addressed

Conclusion	Warning	FYI	Future	Current	TBD
(Circle			(Prophetic)		
One):			Past		

Prayer Points

1.

2.

3.

30-Day Dream Interpretation Journal

DATE:
Easy Recall Title:
Observation & Action:

People: **Animal:** **Place:**

Event: **Number:** **Color:**

Emotion/Feeling (Circle One): Fearful/Scared Angry Happy Sad

Worried Confused Neutral Peaceful Other:

Focus: Me Someone Else - Who? Thing – What?

Relatable Context in Life:

Interpretation:

Recurring Good Dream? = Certainty Chances Increases
Recurring Bad Dream? = Not Properly Addressed

Conclusion (Circle One): Warning FYI Future (Prophetic) Past Current TBD

Prayer Points

1.

2.

3.

DREAMS

DATE:
Easy Recall Title:
Observation & Action:

People: **Animal:**   **Place:**

Event: **Number:**   **Color:**

Emotion/Feeling   Fearful   Angry   Happy   Sad
(Circle One):   /Scared

Worried   Confused   Neutral   Peaceful   Other:

Focus: Me   Someone Else -   Thing – What?
                               Who?

Relatable Context in Life:

Interpretation:

Recurring Good Dream? = Certainty Chances Increases
Recurring Bad Dream? = Not Properly Addressed

Conclusion   Warning   FYI   Future   Current   TBD
(Circle   (Prophetic)
One):   Past

Prayer Points

1.

2.

3.

30-Day Dream Interpretation Journal

DATE:
Easy Recall Title:
Observation & Action:

People: **Animal:** **Place:**

Event: **Number:** **Color:**

Emotion/Feeling (Circle One): Fearful/Scared Angry Happy Sad

Worried Confused Neutral Peaceful Other:

Focus: Me Someone Else - Who? Thing – What?

Relatable Context in Life:

Interpretation:

Recurring Good Dream? = Certainty Chances Increases
Recurring Bad Dream? = Not Properly Addressed

Conclusion (Circle One): Warning FYI Future (Prophetic) Past Current TBD

Prayer Points

1.

2.

3.

DREAMS

DATE:
Easy Recall Title:
Observation & Action:

People:　　　　　　　　**Animal:**　　　　　　　　**Place:**

Event:　　　　　　　　**Number:**　　　　　　　　**Color:**

Emotion/Feeling　Fearful　　　　Angry　　　　Happy　　　　Sad
(Circle One):　　/Scared

　Worried　　　　Confused　　　　Neutral　　　　Peaceful　　　　Other:

Focus:　　　　Me　　　　Someone Else -　　　　Thing – What?
　　　　　　　　　　　　　Who?

Relatable Context in Life:

Interpretation:

Recurring Good Dream? = Certainty Chances Increases

Recurring Bad Dream? = Not Properly Addressed

Conclusion　Warning　　FYI　　Future　　　　Current　　TBD
(Circle　　　　　　　　　　　　(Prophetic)
One):　　　　　　　　　　　　　Past

Prayer Points

1.

2.

3.

30-Day Dream Interpretation Journal

DATE:
Easy Recall Title:
Observation & Action:

People: **Animal:**   **Place:**

Event: **Number:**   **Color:**

Emotion/Feeling   Fearful   Angry   Happy   Sad
(Circle One):   /Scared

Worried   Confused   Neutral   Peaceful   Other:

Focus: Me   Someone Else -   Thing – What?
                                  Who?

Relatable Context in Life:

Interpretation:

Recurring Good Dream? = Certainty Chances Increases
Recurring Bad Dream? = Not Properly Addressed

Conclusion   Warning   FYI   Future   Current   TBD
(Circle   (Prophetic)
One):   Past

Prayer Points

1.

2.

3.

158

DREAMS

DATE:
Easy Recall Title:
Observation & Action:

People: **Animal:**   **Place:**

Event: **Number:**   **Color:**

Emotion/Feeling   Fearful   Angry   Happy   Sad
(Circle One):   /Scared

Worried   Confused   Neutral   Peaceful   Other:

Focus: Me   Someone Else -   Thing – What?
                            Who?

Relatable Context in Life:

Interpretation:

Recurring Good Dream? = Certainty Chances Increases
Recurring Bad Dream? = Not Properly Addressed

Conclusion   Warning   FYI   Future   Current   TBD
(Circle   (Prophetic)
One):   Past

Prayer Points

1.

2.

3.

30-Day Dream Interpretation Journal

DATE:
Easy Recall Title:
Observation & Action:

People: **Animal:**   **Place:**

Event: **Number:**   **Color:**

Emotion/Feeling   Fearful   Angry   Happy   Sad
(Circle One):   /Scared

Worried   Confused   Neutral   Peaceful   Other:

Focus: Me   Someone Else -   Thing – What?
                                 Who?

Relatable Context in Life:

Interpretation:

Recurring Good Dream? = Certainty Chances Increases

Recurring Bad Dream? = Not Properly Addressed

Conclusion	Warning	FYI	Future	Current	TBD
(Circle			(Prophetic)		
One):			Past		

Prayer Points

1.

2.

3.

DREAMS

DATE:
Easy Recall Title:
Observation & Action:

People:　　　　　　　**Animal:**　　　　　　　**Place:**

Event:　　　　　　　**Number:**　　　　　　　**Color:**

Emotion/Feeling　Fearful　　　Angry　　　Happy　　　Sad
(Circle One):　　/Scared

Worried　　　Confused　　　Neutral　　　Peaceful　　　Other:

Focus:　　　Me　　　Someone Else -　　　Thing – What?
　　　　　　　　　　　Who?

Relatable Context in Life:

Interpretation:

Recurring Good Dream? = Certainty Chances Increases
Recurring Bad Dream? = Not Properly Addressed

Conclusion　Warning　FYI　Future　　　Current　TBD
(Circle　　　　　　　　　(Prophetic)
One):　　　　　　　　　　Past

Prayer Points

1.

2.

3.

161

30-Day Dream Interpretation Journal

DATE:
Easy Recall Title:
Observation & Action:

People: **Animal:**   **Place:**

Event: **Number:**   **Color:**

Emotion/Feeling   Fearful   Angry   Happy   Sad
(Circle One):   /Scared

Worried   Confused   Neutral   Peaceful   Other:

Focus: Me   Someone Else -   Thing – What?
                                 Who?

Relatable Context in Life:

Interpretation:

Recurring Good Dream? = Certainty Chances Increases
Recurring Bad Dream? = Not Properly Addressed

Conclusion   Warning   FYI   Future   Current   TBD
(Circle   (Prophetic)
One):   Past

Prayer Points

1.

2.

3.

DREAMS

DATE:
Easy Recall Title:
Observation & Action:

People: **Animal:**   **Place:**

Event: **Number:**   **Color:**

Emotion/Feeling   Fearful   Angry   Happy   Sad
(Circle One):   /Scared

Worried   Confused   Neutral   Peaceful   Other:

Focus: Me   Someone Else -   Thing – What?
                             Who?

Relatable Context in Life:

Interpretation:

Recurring Good Dream? = Certainty Chances Increases
Recurring Bad Dream? = Not Properly Addressed

Conclusion   Warning   FYI   Future   Current   TBD
(Circle   (Prophetic)
One):   Past

Prayer Points

1.

2.

3.

30-Day Dream Interpretation Journal

DATE:
Easy Recall Title:
Observation & Action:

People:　　　　　　**Animal:**　　　　　　**Place:**

Event:　　　　　　**Number:**　　　　　　**Color:**

Emotion/Feeling　Fearful　　　Angry　　　Happy　　　Sad
(Circle One):　　/Scared

Worried　　　Confused　　　Neutral　　　Peaceful　　　Other:

Focus:　　　Me　　　Someone Else -　　　Thing – What?
　　　　　　　　　　　Who?

Relatable Context in Life:

Interpretation:

Recurring Good Dream? = Certainty Chances Increases
Recurring Bad Dream? = Not Properly Addressed

Conclusion　Warning　　FYI　　Future　　　Current　　TBD
(Circle　　　　　　　　　　　(Prophetic)
One):　　　　　　　　　　　　Past

Prayer Points

1.

2.

3.

DREAMS

DATE:
Easy Recall Title:
Observation & Action:

People: **Animal:**   **Place:**

Event: **Number:**   **Color:**

Emotion/Feeling   Fearful   Angry   Happy   Sad
(Circle One):   /Scared

Worried   Confused   Neutral   Peaceful   Other:

Focus: Me   Someone Else -   Thing – What?
                                   Who?

Relatable Context in Life:

Interpretation:

Recurring Good Dream? = Certainty Chances Increases
Recurring Bad Dream? = Not Properly Addressed

Conclusion   Warning   FYI   Future   Current   TBD
(Circle   (Prophetic)
One):   Past

Prayer Points

1.

2.

3.

30-Day Dream Interpretation Journal

DATE:
Easy Recall Title:
Observation & Action:

People: **Animal:**   **Place:**

Event: **Number:**   **Color:**

Emotion/Feeling   Fearful   Angry   Happy   Sad
(Circle One):   /Scared

Worried   Confused   Neutral   Peaceful   Other:

Focus: Me   Someone Else -   Thing – What?
                             Who?

Relatable Context in Life:

Interpretation:

Recurring Good Dream? = Certainty Chances Increases

Recurring Bad Dream? = Not Properly Addressed

| **Conclusion (Circle One):** | Warning | FYI | Future (Prophetic) Past | Current | TBD |

Prayer Points

1.

2.

3.

DREAMS

DATE:
Easy Recall Title:
Observation & Action:

People: **Animal:**   **Place:**

Event: **Number:**   **Color:**

Emotion/Feeling   Fearful   Angry   Happy   Sad
(Circle One):   /Scared

Worried   Confused   Neutral   Peaceful   Other:

Focus: Me   Someone Else - Who?   Thing – What?

Relatable Context in Life:

Interpretation:

Recurring Good Dream? = Certainty Chances Increases
Recurring Bad Dream? = Not Properly Addressed

Conclusion   Warning   FYI   Future   Current   TBD
(Circle   (Prophetic)
One):   Past

Prayer Points

1.

2.

3.

30-Day Dream Interpretation Journal

DATE:
Easy Recall Title:
Observation & Action:

People: **Animal:** **Place:**

Event: **Number:** **Color:**

Emotion/Feeling Fearful Angry Happy Sad
(Circle One): /Scared

Worried Confused Neutral Peaceful Other:

Focus: Me Someone Else - Thing – What?
Who?

Relatable Context in Life:

Interpretation:

Recurring Good Dream? = Certainty Chances Increases
Recurring Bad Dream? = Not Properly Addressed

Conclusion	Warning	FYI	Future	Current	TBD
(Circle			(Prophetic)		
One):			Past		

Prayer Points

1.

2.

3.

DREAMS

DATE:
Easy Recall Title:
Observation & Action:

People: **Animal:**   **Place:**

Event: **Number:**   **Color:**

Emotion/Feeling Fearful   Angry   Happy   Sad
(Circle One):   /Scared

Worried   Confused   Neutral   Peaceful   Other:

Focus: Me   Someone Else -   Thing – What?
                            Who?

Relatable Context in Life:

Interpretation:

Recurring Good Dream? = Certainty Chances Increases
Recurring Bad Dream? = Not Properly Addressed

Conclusion   Warning   FYI   Future   Current   TBD
(Circle   (Prophetic)
One):   Past

Prayer Points

1.

2.

3.

30-Day Dream Interpretation Journal

DATE:
Easy Recall Title:
Observation & Action:

People: **Animal:**   **Place:**

Event: **Number:**   **Color:**

Emotion/Feeling (Circle One):   Fearful/Scared   Angry   Happy   Sad

Worried   Confused   Neutral   Peaceful   Other:

Focus: Me   Someone Else - Who?   Thing – What?

Relatable Context in Life:

Interpretation:

Recurring Good Dream? = Certainty Chances Increases

Recurring Bad Dream? = Not Properly Addressed

Conclusion (Circle One):   Warning   FYI   Future (Prophetic) Past   Current   TBD

Prayer Points

1.

2.

3.

DREAMS

DATE:
Easy Recall Title:
Observation & Action:

People: **Animal:**   **Place:**

Event: **Number:**   **Color:**

Emotion/Feeling   Fearful   Angry   Happy   Sad
(Circle One):   /Scared

Worried   Confused   Neutral   Peaceful   Other:

Focus: Me   Someone Else - Who?   Thing – What?

Relatable Context in Life:

Interpretation:

Recurring Good Dream? = Certainty Chances Increases
Recurring Bad Dream? = Not Properly Addressed

Conclusion   Warning   FYI   Future   Current   TBD
(Circle   (Prophetic)
One):   Past

Prayer Points

1.

2.

3.

30-Day Dream Interpretation Journal

DATE:
Easy Recall Title:
Observation & Action:

People: **Animal:**   **Place:**

Event: **Number:**   **Color:**

Emotion/Feeling   Fearful   Angry   Happy   Sad
(Circle One):   /Scared

Worried   Confused   Neutral   Peaceful   Other:

Focus: Me   Someone Else -   Thing – What?
                                Who?

Relatable Context in Life:

Interpretation:

Recurring Good Dream? = Certainty Chances Increases
Recurring Bad Dream? = Not Properly Addressed

Conclusion   Warning   FYI   Future   Current   TBD
(Circle   (Prophetic)
One):   Past

Prayer Points

1.

2.

3.

DREAMS

DATE:
Easy Recall Title:
Observation & Action:

People: **Animal:**   **Place:**

Event: **Number:**   **Color:**

Emotion/Feeling   Fearful   Angry   Happy   Sad
(Circle One):   /Scared

Worried   Confused   Neutral   Peaceful   Other:

Focus: Me   Someone Else -   Thing – What?
                                  Who?

Relatable Context in Life:

Interpretation:

Recurring Good Dream? = Certainty Chances Increases

Recurring Bad Dream? = Not Properly Addressed

Conclusion   Warning   FYI   Future   Current   TBD
(Circle   (Prophetic)
One):   Past

Prayer Points

1.

2.

3.

30-Day Dream Interpretation Journal

DATE:
Easy Recall Title:
Observation & Action:

People: **Animal:**   **Place:**

Event: **Number:**   **Color:**

Emotion/Feeling   Fearful   Angry   Happy   Sad
(Circle One):   /Scared

Worried   Confused   Neutral   Peaceful   Other:

Focus: Me   Someone Else -   Thing – What?
                              Who?

Relatable Context in Life:

Interpretation:

Recurring Good Dream? = Certainty Chances Increases

Recurring Bad Dream? = Not Properly Addressed

Conclusion   Warning   FYI   Future   Current   TBD
(Circle   (Prophetic)
One):   Past

Prayer Points

1.

2.

3.

DREAMS

DATE:
Easy Recall Title:
Observation & Action:

People: **Animal:**   **Place:**

Event: **Number:**   **Color:**

Emotion/Feeling   Fearful   Angry   Happy   Sad
(Circle One):   /Scared

Worried   Confused   Neutral   Peaceful   Other:

Focus: Me   Someone Else -   Thing – What?
                            Who?

Relatable Context in Life:

Interpretation:

Recurring Good Dream? = Certainty Chances Increases
Recurring Bad Dream? = Not Properly Addressed

Conclusion   Warning   FYI   Future   Current   TBD
(Circle   (Prophetic)
One):   Past

Prayer Points

1.

2.

3.

30-Day Dream Interpretation Journal

DATE:
Easy Recall Title:
Observation & Action:

People:　　　　　　**Animal:**　　　　　　**Place:**

Event:　　　　　　**Number:**　　　　　　**Color:**

Emotion/Feeling　Fearful　　Angry　　Happy　　Sad
(Circle One):　　/Scared

Worried　　　Confused　　Neutral　　Peaceful　　Other:

Focus:　　　Me　　　Someone Else -　　Thing – What?
　　　　　　　　　　　Who?

Relatable Context in Life:

Interpretation:

Recurring Good Dream? = Certainty Chances Increases
Recurring Bad Dream? = Not Properly Addressed

Conclusion　Warning　　FYI　　Future　　　Current　　TBD
(Circle　　　　　　　　　　　(Prophetic)
One):　　　　　　　　　　　　Past

Prayer Points

1.

2.

3.

DREAMS

DATE:
Easy Recall Title:
Observation & Action:

People: **Animal:**   **Place:**

Event: **Number:**   **Color:**

Emotion/Feeling   Fearful   Angry   Happy   Sad
(Circle One):   /Scared

Worried   Confused   Neutral   Peaceful   Other:

Focus: Me   Someone Else -   Thing – What?
                            Who?

Relatable Context in Life:

Interpretation:

Recurring Good Dream? = Certainty Chances Increases
Recurring Bad Dream? = Not Properly Addressed

Conclusion   Warning   FYI   Future   Current   TBD
(Circle   (Prophetic)
One):   Past

Prayer Points

1.

2.

3.

30-Day Dream Interpretation Journal

DATE:
Easy Recall Title:
Observation & Action:

People: **Animal:**   **Place:**

Event: **Number:**   **Color:**

Emotion/Feeling   Fearful   Angry   Happy   Sad
(Circle One):   /Scared

Worried   Confused   Neutral   Peaceful   Other:

Focus: Me   Someone Else -   Thing – What?
                        Who?

Relatable Context in Life:

Interpretation:

Recurring Good Dream? = Certainty Chances Increases
Recurring Bad Dream? = Not Properly Addressed

Conclusion   Warning   FYI   Future   Current   TBD
**(Circle   (Prophetic)
One):**   Past

Prayer Points

1.

2.

3.

DREAMS

DATE:
Easy Recall Title:
Observation & Action:

People: **Animal:** **Place:**

Event: **Number:** **Color:**

Emotion/Feeling (Circle One): Fearful/Scared   Angry   Happy   Sad

Worried   Confused   Neutral   Peaceful   Other:

Focus: Me   Someone Else - Who?   Thing – What?

Relatable Context in Life:

Interpretation:

Recurring Good Dream? = Certainty Chances Increases
Recurring Bad Dream? = Not Properly Addressed

Conclusion (Circle One): Warning   FYI   Future (Prophetic) Past   Current   TBD

Prayer Points

1.

2.

3.

BOOKS BY OLA ABINA

Ola wrote this book for anyone who wants to stop anxiety, overthinking, self-doubt, negativity, and depression for good. Even as a Christian, with a forced smile, he went through dark times and considered ending his life. He experienced intense pain and cried hopelessly every night until he found a solution. From his experience, he shares how to reclaim one's life. This devotional covers 40 various topics like loving yourself, healing trust issues, finding emotional healing, understanding God when life doesn't make sense, creating daily morning routines for success etc.

Ola decided to change his financial life after a tragic event forever altered his path for life. With just a few days until his twentieth year at work, he left. He didn't retire. He left. No pension or retirement check safety net. He left his $170,000-per-year job. In this very concise book, Ola created a five-step blueprint that helped him secure financial freedom. The book also reveals the spiritual secret that every person who becomes rich has and how you can tap into it. Starting with basic concepts, you'll learn how to assess your current situation, identify areas of improvement, and start putting plans into action right away. You strive for financial freedom. But how do you get there? This book provides an answer.

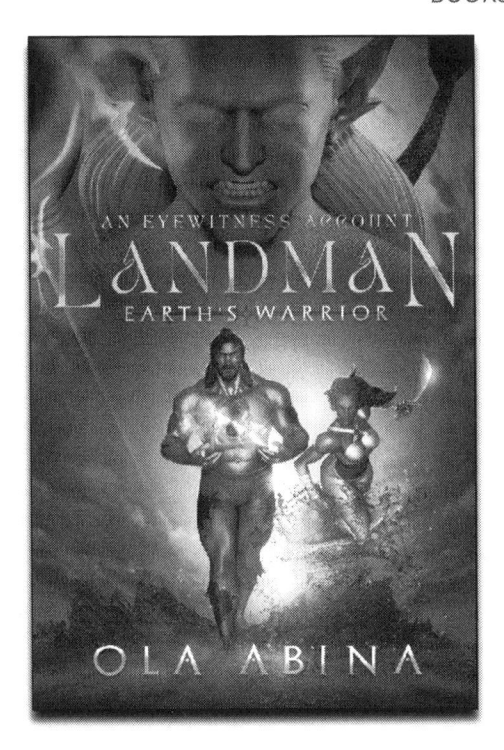

"I have a plan to overthrow the Creator." Gasps spread throughout the audience of angels. Many whispered he would never win, and the Creator would not allow it."

In this thrilling novel, immerse yourself in an intense battle for power and control as Rogue, an ambitious archangel, sets his sights on the Creator's throne. With charm and persuasion, he successfully gathers a formidable army of angels ready to act. However, amidst this divine conflict, there is an unlikely hero, the Landman, who finds himself unwittingly caught in the crossfire. Unbeknownst to him, the Landman holds the key to altering the course of this war. Join him on a journey filled with suspense, thrilling battles, and the ultimate test of courage. Will the Landman rise to the challenge and become the hero mankind desperately needs? Find out in this captivating tale that will keep you on the edge of your seat.

Discover the keys to financial freedom through time-tested biblical principles and cutting-edge strategies! Accelerate your journey to prosperity by learning how to:

- Generate wealth even in times of crisis.
- Apply financial principles that lead to abundance.
- Break free from the shackles of debt.
- Stay ahead of the game by identifying future trends in products and services! Unlock the secrets to a prosperous future and secure your financial well-being today!

Discover a book that brings hope, empowerment, and healing. Whether you're a victim of your own choices, the actions of others, or simply the unpredictable journey of life itself, this powerful resource offers hope and solace. With engaging stories and powerful insights, this resource is a must-have for anyone who has faced adversity, is currently navigating challenging times, or will inevitably encounter obstacles in the future. Get ready to embrace a dynamic blueprint for facing life's toughest trials, emerging victoriously and stronger than ever before, where every obstacle becomes an opportunity for growth.

ABOUT THE AUTHOR

Olaoluwa "Ola" Abina, most widely known for his international best seller, *42 Financial Independence Laws,* is an author, publisher, and a well sought after conference speaker. Ola's writing journey began after the sudden demise of his beloved mother, which debuted his first book *Save Me From This Hour – Overcoming Life's Adversities.* In response to overwhelming demand from him for life advice, and dealing with the same issues himself, Ola found a passion for writing on topics about overcoming life's challenges, love, financial freedom and relationships using time-tested biblical solutions. After leaving his full-time job in 2021 to pursue his purpose of becoming a full-time author, Ola released the following books *Landman Earth's Warrior (A work of fiction) and 2023:ROAD TO A MILLION.* His last book, *Before I Give Up*, quickly rocketed to success and sold out within a few weeks. Ola's uniqueness lies

About The Author

in using the name and principles of Jesus Christ to solve contemporary problems. As he travels around the world, using these principles, he has seen the lives of hundreds of thousands transformed as he inspires men and women, becoming a voice of hope to those who have lost faith. Ola is the host of "Jesus Is Too Real," a program that uses the name and principles to solve contemporary problems. He currently resides with his family in Baltimore, Maryland.

You can connect with Ola on these platforms:

Instagram - @Officialjitr
Facebook – Jesusistooreal
Tiktok - @OfficialJesusistooreal
YouTube – JITRONYOUTUBE

Email - ola@jesusistooreal.com

Made in the USA
Columbia, SC
03 January 2025